A NEW BIRTH
OF
FREEDOM

Dear Mr. Howlett:

Thank you for your early support.
With your continued help, we will
win!

Cordially,

1311/10016

A NEW
BIRTH
OF
FREEDOM

VISION FOR AMERICA

STEVE FORBES

 REGNERY
PUBLISHING, INC.

Since 1947 • An Eagle Publishing Company

Library of Congress Cataloging-in-Publication Data

Forbes, Steve, 1947–
    A new birth of freedom / by Steve Forbes.
       p.   cm.
    Includes index.
    ISBN 0–89526–320–3
    1. United States—Politics and government—1993– 2. United States—Social conditions—1980– 3. Forbes, Steve, 1947– —Political and social views. I. Title.
E885.F67   1999
973.929—dc21   99–35791
                                                      CIP

Published in the United States by
Regnery Publishing, Inc.
An Eagle Publishing Company
One Massachusetts Avenue, NW
Washington, DC 20001

Distributed to the trade by
National Book Network
4720-A Boston Way
Lanham, MD 20706

Paid for by Forbes2000, Inc.

Printed on acid-free paper
Manufactured in the United States of America

10 9 8 7 6 5 4 3 2 1

Books are available in quantity for promotional or premium use. Write to Director of Special Sales, Regnery Publishing, Inc., One Massachusetts Avenue, NW, Washington, DC 20001, for information on discounts and terms or call (202) 216–0600.

To my wife,
Sabina,
and our five daughters,
Roberta, Sabina, Catherine, Moira, and Elizabeth.

CONTENTS

"…We here highly resolve that these dead shall not have died in vain; that this nation, under God, shall have a new birth of freedom…"

—President Abraham Lincoln at Gettysburg

INTRODUCTION

I DON'T BELIEVE in business as usual, and I don't believe in politics as usual. But I hadn't been planning to run for president.

I was busy with the magazine *Forbes*, where I'd taken over the helm after my father died in 1990. We were just beginning to pull ahead of *Business Week*, our biggest competitor, and we had recently launched a new high-tech magazine for the general reader, *Forbes ASAP*, to tell the stories of the people creating the new Information Age economy. My only serious excursions in politics at that time had been helping my friends Jack Kemp and Bill Bennett map out and promote innovative new strategies of economic freedom and cultural renewal at a grassroots organization called Empower America, and helping craft a dramatic 30 percent across-the-board tax-cut proposal to revive the economy and help working families in my home state of New Jersey. The tax cuts were soon enacted into law.

So in the summer of 1995 my mind was more on growing our family business than on politics. But as I watched the Republican primary candidates begin to stake out their positions, I became more and more concerned. Our party had undergone a strange transformation since Ronald Reagan left office in 1989. It was almost as if Reagan's passion for changing America—unleashing the genius of the American people to create new jobs and small businesses; and putting the United States onto a path of technological leadership—and his passion for changing the world by winning a

peaceful victory over our Cold War adversary of forty years, the
Soviet Union, had been wiped from the Republican Party's collec-
tive memory. Not one of our front-running candidates was talking
about what the end of the Cold War meant for America and the
world. Not one was offering new ideas to take money and power out
of the hands of the Washington politicians and truly put it back in
the hands of the American people. No one seemed to be offering
positive, forward-looking solutions to help families and small business owners being harassed by the Internal Revenue Service, seniors
worried about the future of Social Security, workers getting crushed
by massive payroll taxes with little to show for it, children trapped in
dangerous and failing inner–city schools, and millions of Americans
living without the security of having real health insurance. No one
was talking about how to help countries newly liberated from Soviet
domination sink deep roots into the soil of democratic capitalism
and experience the power of free markets and free elections. Nor was
anyone talking about the serious new threats that lay just over the
horizon.

It was surreal. America was poised to enter the greatest era of
economic freedom and spiritual renewal the world had ever seen.
But as I surveyed the political landscape in 1995, it was pretty clear
that the Washington political culture didn't get it. Were we to be
condemned by future generations as an era of missed opportunities?

As a new arrival to these shores in the first part of the century, my
grandfather marveled at the wide-open opportunity in America—
so different from the grinding limits in his native Scotland. He
made his living at first as a freelance journalist, often writing about
the businessmen and entrepreneurs of the era. But after a few years
he thought, "Why just write about it? Why not start a business
myself?" And so, in 1917, *Forbes* magazine was born.

In the summer of 1995 I asked myself a similar question. As
chairman of the board that oversaw Radio Free Europe and Radio
Liberty under President Reagan, and as editor-in-chief of *Forbes*, I'd
spent much of my time traveling the United States and the world,

meeting with leaders in business and government and covering the enormous social, political, and economic changes under way at home and abroad. For three decades, I had sought out American and international entrepreneurs and innovators and written about the people and ideas shaping the future. But what bothered me was that I saw no such spirit of innovation and change in Washington right at the moment of maximum opportunity for America and the world. So, I thought, instead of just standing on the sidelines, commenting on events, why not get involved myself?

America is poised to enter the greatest era of economic freedom and spiritual renewal the world has ever seen.

To call such an undertaking immense would be an understatement. The fall before an election year is about as late as you can get to announce for president. Most candidates these days start putting together their organizations, building bridges of relationships, and laying the groundwork a year or two before an election year. The Iowa caucuses were only a few months away and New Hampshire's primary was not long after that. Half my friends told me running for president was crazy, but I knew that already. The other half told me that *I* was crazy. But my wife, Sabina, assured me this was not the case—at least no more than usual. And she and our five daughters (along with my sister and three brothers and their families), though not eager for the national spotlight, said that if I thought it was this important, they would support me all the way.

From the beginning it was a seat-of-the-pants operation, but innumerable volunteers and committed workers flocked to our headquarters in New Jersey, and what we lacked in organization, we made up for in spirit. We made a lot of mistakes, but I felt proud that we got a few essential things right. Most of the other primary candidates, who in the beginning couldn't find enough bad things to say about my flat tax proposal, sooner or later came out with versions of their own. Our positive, forward-looking message of hope, growth, and opportunity seemed to capture the imagination of the

American people. We landed on the cover of *Time* and *Newsweek*; won two stunning, come-from-behind primary victories in Delaware and Arizona; and gave our front-runner and soon-to-be nominee, Bob Dole, a respectable run. Eventually, Senator Dole himself embraced an ambitious tax-cut proposal and Colin Powell declared the Republicans "the pro-growth party."

My only regret is that, jumping so late into the race, I wasn't able to get my message across as fully as I would have liked. Trying to run a presidential campaign is a little like driving a freight train while you're still building the tracks. Trying to communicate new ideas in a hostile media environment is a little like trying to talk underwater. By hammering away incessantly on the flat tax, I was able to force the party's attention back to the crucial issue of economic opportunity and growth, but my wider message of personal freedom and hope for America's future often seemed to get lost in the fog of battle. I have always felt that tax cuts are only secondarily an economic issue. Tax cuts are a means, not an end, by giving back to the American people the resources that will enable them to take control of their own lives. At its heart, the new birth of freedom that I am proposing in these pages has to do with the essential things that make the American experiment in democracy the "last, best hope of earth"—a belief that each individual, each life, is a unique creation, infinitely valuable to God, and worthy of the full security and dignity that can be found only in freedom.

One of the great things about representative democracy is that it is a two-way education. It's not just a candidate telling people what he or she thinks. It's people telling the candidate what *they* think: their aspirations, their dreams, their concerns. For me, the greatest gift of the last campaign was the opportunity to get to know so many fascinating and wonderful people and see them respond so enthusiastically to an honest, substantive message from a novice messenger. It belied the conventional wisdom that people have succumbed to an age of sound-bite politics where spin trumps substance. The American people are much smarter than the media

elites give them credit for. America is a land made up of seemingly
ordinary people doing extraordinary things. They work hard at their
jobs, help the less fortunate, try to improve their schools, build their
communities, and come together in reverent thanks for all the blessings that have been bestowed on this great nation. The goodwill and
generosity of so many Americans are truly
astonishing and heartening. They want to be **My goal is to show**
treated with dignity and respect. They aren't **how we can launch a**
afraid of new ideas, even big ideas—even if **new birth of freedom**
the messenger is an outsider and not part of **that will help all**
the establishment. In fact, in my conversations **Americans achieve**
with people during the 1996 campaign and **their dreams—just as**
since then, I find that people are profoundly **my grandfather**
disappointed and turned off by politics-as- **achieved his when he**
usual. They don't want sizzle; they want steak. **came to this country.**
Who can blame them? They realize that
political spin is substance abuse. This is, after
all, America, and whether it's in business or in politics, Americans
expect a square deal. If they don't get it, they move on. When
famous brand names keep offering familiar bland products, look
out: people are headed for the exits.

My goal with this book is to show how we can launch a new birth
of freedom that will help all Americans achieve their dreams—just
as my grandfather achieved his when he came to this country as a
Scottish immigrant, the sixth in a family of ten children, with barely
a grade-school education and practically no money.

My great-grandfather was raised by a single mother. He grew to
become a shopkeeper, tailor, husband, and father—and as my
grandfather told me, "there were more children than funds." So at
the age of fourteen my grandfather left school forever and took a job
as a "printer's devil," taught himself shorthand, and worked his way
to becoming a reporter when he was sixteen for the paper in
Aberdeen, then eventually came to America in the first years of the
twentieth century.

Living in New York (he would eventually move to New Jersey after getting married), B.C. Forbes continued in journalism, writing for newspapers and magazines. He became a noted financial columnist for the Hearst newspapers, arguably then America's most powerful chain. He was a tireless digger of facts and a prolific writer. Always outspoken in his views, he became increasingly frustrated when editors couldn't use everything that he wrote. It offended his frugal Scottish nature: "All that good information going to waste!" he would say. So in 1917, the same year as the Communist Revolution in Russia, he decided to become an entrepreneur himself and founded *Forbes* magazine to tell the stories of the men and women building the greatest economy on the face of the planet. His credo, which appeared in the very first issue of *Forbes* on September 15, 1917, has continued to guide the magazine, and is something I have come to embrace as well. He wrote:

Business was originated to produce happiness, not to pile up millions.

Are we in danger of forgetting this?

Too often in talking with so-called "successful" men I cannot but feel that they are making business an end and an aim in itself, that they regard the multiplying of their millions and the extension of their works as the be-all and end-all of life, life itself.

Such men are sometimes happy in a feverish hustling sort of way, much as a fly placed in a tube of oxygen is furiously happy until its life burns out.

But they have no time for the tranquil, finer, deeper joys of living. They are so obsessed with the material that they cannot enjoy the immaterial, the intangible, the ideal, the spiritual—quiet thought, self-communion, reflection, poise, inward happiness, domestic felicity, an evening of conversation on the things that do not pass, sober self-analysis conducive to unselfish human service.

What profiteth a man to gain uncounted riches if he thereby sacrifices his better self, his nobler qualities of manhood?

Mere getting is not living.

The man who depends upon his bank account to insure him a happy life reaps disappointment.

Success is, or should be, the ambition of each one of us.

To the painter, success is to be acclaimed justly as a great artist. To the author, success is to be recognized as a great writer, a truthful interpreter of human nature.

To the businessman, success heretofore, too often has been merely to become rich.

That is not a high standard. It is a standard, happily, that is passing.

My grandfather was a devout believer in democratic, free-market capitalism, but he never thought of it as the "aim" and "be-all and end-all" of life. He spoke often of business as a creative enterprise. More than just making money, it was about adding to the sum of human happiness. Business must have a soul, or it is ultimately empty. The head of each of his "Fact and Comment" columns in the magazine carried this biblical admonition from Proverbs to the businessmen he covered every day as a journalist: "With all thy getting, get understanding."

It was advice that served him well. In 1928 America's leading media mogul, William Randolph Hearst, offered my grandfather the equivalent today of tens of millions of dollars in cash to buy *Forbes*, the only general business magazine in America at that time. My grandfather said no. He wanted to remain free and independent. The next year, the stock market crashed, the Great Depression began, and *Forbes* almost went under. For years, my grandfather struggled to keep it afloat, unable to cash his own paychecks because there was never enough money in the bank. It was a vivid reminder that life is not measured by the cash in our pockets but by the content of our character. Riches are fleeting. All we really have to hold onto in this life are our values and education, our family and faith, and our sense of purpose and direction. It is these that guide us through the tough times. One minute my grandfather was at the top; the next minute a lifetime of professional work was crashing around him. But he never lost his bearings. Adversity brought out the best in him. Eventually, the economy began to pick up again, and the magazine survived.

"With all thy getting, get understanding." It is a tradition we have kept at the magazine to this day. And for me, I have sought to understand not just what makes great companies, but what makes great countries. What is the essence of the American experiment in freedom, and how can we make it work for everyone, especially those who feel like they are being left behind?

Just as my grandfather knew that life isn't just about acquiring money and material possessions, in our hearts we know that there is more to being an American than simply taking up space in one particular corner of the planet. Being an American is a commitment to individual freedom and social progress.

In this century, freedom and progress were hard fought and dearly won victories that included world wars against fascism and a cold war against communism. As we head into a new century—indeed, a new millennium—I believe that we are at a turning point in man's long struggle to be free. The world is looking to us for an example of how to adapt to changing times and circumstances. If America gets it right, the rest of the world has a chance to get it right. But if America gets in trouble, the rest of the world is going to be in serious trouble as well.

I have sought to understand not just what makes great companies, but what makes great countries.

I'm an optimist. I don't accept the whinings of those who say that America's best days are behind us, that we are doomed for economic decline, cultural collapse, environmental apocalypse, and international irrelevancy. It could happen, of course, without effective leadership. But it is hardly our destiny. The truth is that we can experience a new birth of freedom. In the pages ahead I will explain why and how.

CHAPTER ONE

IMAGINE

ON NOVEMBER 18, 1863, a tall, lanky man with a silk top hat arrived at the railroad station in Gettysburg, Pennsylvania. The next day he would stand on a battlefield of war and give one of the most heralded speeches ever delivered, a two-minute oration honoring the brave soldiers who gave their lives on that soil for America's future. Abraham Lincoln concluded that speech with words that have become a priceless part of our national legacy: "We here highly resolve that these dead shall not have died in vain; that this nation, under God, shall have a new birth of freedom; and that government of the people, by the people, for the people, shall not perish from the earth."

Freedom is the central theme of American history, the heart of what the American experiment is all about. Our country has experienced a new birth of freedom more than once in its history: at its dawn, with our victory in the War of Independence; in the Civil War, which insured the nation's unity and ended the scourge of slavery forever; in the Progressive Movement at the turn of the century, which curbed the excesses of both industry and government; in

Wherever I go, I find Americans who do not feel free.

the Allied victory during World War II, which insured the security of America and made the dream of freedom possible for millions around the globe; and in the civil rights movement, which won for America's black citizens the equal rights and full citizenship they long had been denied. Most recently, the determined stand of the United States and our allies against communism during more than forty years of Cold War brought about a new birth of freedom in Eastern Europe, while insuring the victory of free peoples over one of the greatest threats that they had ever faced.

As we head into a new century and a new millennium, America again yearns for a new birth of freedom. Big government and faceless bureaucracies continue to encroach upon fundamental American rights and freedoms. Taxes rise inexorably despite endless promises by the politicians to hold the line. Our economy is prospering but many Americans feel they are falling even further behind. We face no superpower rivalry but our security is eroding as America's armed forces have been downsized and numerous dictators are developing weapons of mass destruction—nuclear, chemical, and biological—that could kill as many Americans as any war of the past. We also face serious problems with drug addiction, youth gangs, violence in our schools, and family disintegration—all trends that rob human beings of their freedoms and threaten to weaken our social fabric.

Americans today are searching for a better life, a life of enhanced personal freedom, moral values, a sense of community, and shared prosperity for all. We no longer believe that material things alone lead to happiness. We want to rediscover the things that matter most, starting within the walls of our own homes. We want the next century to be a time of new beginnings, a time to start fresh and get our priorities straight. We understand that government alone can never bring us this better life, but we also know that government assuredly can stand in our way.

Why is it that so many Americans today do not feel free?

IS THIS FREEDOM?

Consider the following:

- A family living in Pittsburgh. The father works in a steel mill, as his father did. The mother works part-time while also trying to raise three kids. They earn a decent wage, but despite generally good economic times, they find themselves struggling to make ends meet. It's a task made all the more difficult because they're forced to pay almost half their income to the government in taxes and fees. That's more than they pay for food, clothing, housing, and transportation combined. They feel they are drowning in credit card debt. They are constantly hounded by phone calls from their creditors. Sometimes it feels as if they are on a treadmill—and the treadmill is winning. Are they free?
- A young couple in New Hampshire with one child and one on the way. They work hard, but they're among the forty-three million Americans who don't have health insurance. In their case it's because the husband works for a small manufacturing company that doesn't provide medical coverage and they can't afford coverage on their own. It is a source of great anxiety for this couple. Every night they go to bed worrying about how to pay their doctors and the hospital for the delivery of their next child, and they pray to God they don't get sick themselves. Are they really free?
- Empty-nesters in Georgia rapidly approaching retirement age. They know that Social Security alone isn't going to take care of them, but they look at their weekly paycheck and can't imagine how to squeeze any more out of it to put into savings. Are they really free?
- A fresh-faced high school graduate in Washington, D.C. He applies for his first job, only to discover that despite his new diploma, he doesn't have the reading and math skills necessary to compete and succeed in this new Information Age economy. Is he really free?

- A rancher in Arizona and a farmer in Kansas. They feel pressed to sell the land that's been in their families for generations because of high taxes, suffocating regulations, and the constant erosion of property rights. Are they really free?
- A single mother in Los Angeles. She wants a better life for her children, but sees them trapped in dangerous, failing schools—surrounded by gangs and violence—with no hope, no future, and no way out. Is she really free?
- A couple in Des Moines. They see an explosion of teen drug abuse all around them, and find themselves living with the haunting, private pain of seeing their own children succumb to the same seductions. All around them they see the culture of drugs and violence—what the Pope calls the "culture of death"— glorified in music, in the movies, on television, and on the Internet. Is this really freedom?

The American dream isn't about the accumulation of material things. It is the understanding that we are on this earth to discover—and develop to the fullest—our God-given potential.

Big government did not cause all these problems, but it contributed to them by robbing millions of their self-reliance, making them dependent on handouts. It contributed by subsidizing a bloated educational bureaucracy, while test scores declined steadily. It continues to contribute with high taxes that make it almost impossible for ordinary Americans to get ahead.

There is something fundamentally unfair about a government that takes away so much of people's money, power, and personal control while telling them that life will be better as a result. My friend Lady Thatcher, the former prime minister of Great Britain, calls this the Nanny State. It lectures and scolds its citizenry, all the while taking too much of our money so as to better watch over us, just like a nanny. We can all sympathize with the opinion voiced by Will Rogers: "We're just lucky we're not gettin' all the government we're payin' for!"

Genuine political freedom exists only when the powers of centralized government are limited, checked, controlled, and balanced. As our federal government has grown too large and too powerful, the real loss has been the freedom of people to govern their own lives and participate fully in the American dream.

Never before in human history has a nation occupied the position of influence and strength that America holds today.

To the cynics in Washington, talk of the American dream may seem quaint and trite. But not in my house. We believe in the American dream, because we've had a chance to live it. My wife and I make sure that our girls never take it for granted. From an early age, we set out to teach them that the American dream isn't about the accumulation of material things. It is much deeper and more profound than that. The essence of the American dream is the understanding that we are on this earth and in this land for a higher purpose: to discover—and develop to the fullest—our God-given potential. Anything that stands in the way of the dream, we must fight. Anything that enhances the dream, we must support.

AN UNFAIR SYSTEM

That's what makes the current political culture all the more disturbing. Because even more unfair than the constant erosion of our freedoms to the hand of big government is the way Washington has created a two-tiered system, one for those with money and power and one for those without. Is it really fair for Washington politicians to retire with multimillion-dollar, taxpayer-funded pensions while refusing to lift a finger to save Social Security and give young people the freedom to invest their payroll taxes in their own personal retirement accounts? Is it really fair for federal government employees to have the freedom to choose from a wide variety of health insurance plans tailored to meet their needs, while Washington refuses to remove the onerous restrictions that constantly drive up the cost of health insurance, increase the ranks of the uninsured, and hamper working families from choosing doctors they trust? Is it really fair that the establishment defends a tax system that allows the rich and powerful to hire a small army of lawyers and lobbyists, accountants and advisers to help them reduce their tax bills, but makes life miserable for working families and small business owners who are just trying to get ahead in life?

No, something here is very, very wrong.

As America approaches the dawn of a new century, we face some difficult questions. What good is a balanced federal budget if working families are taxed so heavily that they can't balance their own budgets and are forced deeper and deeper into debt? What good is talking about "saving Social Security" if year after year goes by and nothing ever gets done? What good is "reinventing government" if our children cannot read, are abusing drugs, are having children out of wedlock, and are afraid of violence in school?

Never before in human history has a nation occupied the position of influence and strength that America holds today. Great empires of the past were really regional affairs. Even the Roman Empire was largely confined to the Mediterranean Sea. Today, America's reach is global, not just because of the strength of our economy or the capabilities of the men and women in our armed forces, but because of the example we have set throughout the twentieth century of how free people can adapt to changing times and circumstances.

But, to be blunt: That's not good enough.

Past performance is no guarantee of future success. Anyone in business knows that. "How the mighty have fallen" is a constant theme in the pages of *Forbes* magazine. In fact, of the one hundred largest American companies in 1917, the year my grandfather launched *Forbes,* only fifteen are around today: six oil companies, two automakers, and AT&T, Citicorp, Du Pont, General Electric, Kodak, Procter & Gamble, and Sears. What happened to the other eighty-five companies? Some went bankrupt, some were liquidated, and some were acquired by other companies or simply left in the dust of change. What is true of companies can also be true of countries. The pages of history are littered with the tragic dramas of nations whose leaders would not or could not adapt to change. Just look at the Roman, Spanish, Austrian, and Soviet empires.

Today America is at risk, unless we make some important changes right away.

GETTING BACK ON TRACK—
VISION AND LEADERSHIP

How can great companies and great countries overcome the challenges they face and get back on the track to strength and security? The answer is simple but profound: Honest, visionary leadership that puts principle ahead of personal ambitions. Honest, visionary leadership that does not hesitate to chart new paths, tear down obstacles to progress, and return power to the people. Honest, visionary leadership that believes in the potential of the American people, trusts them to govern themselves, and knows that government possesses no resources save those taken from its productive citizenry.

Honest, sober assessments of past and current conditions, strengths, and weaknesses are essential to successful leadership. If presidents or CEOs start believing their own spin, or become captivated by their own press clips, they risk missing the small but significant signs of change that can spell their demise. Those signs are all around us today—from the Columbine High School massacre, to congressional paralysis on Social Security, to record numbers of military officers leaving the armed forces in disgust. All around we see portents of troubled times ahead for America if fundamental change does not occur.

The importance of vision, sometimes disparaged as the "vision thing," isn't some gimmick to be casually dismissed; it is a gift to be carefully and wisely guarded. Good leaders understand the times in which they live; they can also see "beyond the years." They know where we should be going, why we must get there, and they know how to persuade others to go with them. This is why an obsession with polling is so dangerous. Polls are like a global positioning satellite reference check, not a map. They can tell political or corporate leaders where they are, but they cannot tell them what to do.

This is where our nation's current chief executive and his top deputy fall short. Bewitched and bedazzled by their own spin, they are not being honest about their own shortcomings and blind spots; nor are they preparing America for the storm clouds brewing on the horizon. Today, unemployment and inflation are low, jobs are being created, and the federal budget seems to be in surplus. But that is not the whole picture. The reality behind all the pomp and circumstance of White House photo-ops is troubling. Slowly, without people even realizing it at times, our personal freedoms are being steadily eroded, our educational standards are slipping, our values are under seige, our young people are losing their sense of right and wrong, our economic security is being made vulnerable to a serious global economic crisis, our military is being emasculated, and all around the globe, evil is regrouping, looking for signs of American weakness and lack of resolve.

Instead of addressing these issues, the political leaders we have today largely ignore them. Washington is consumed with special interest lobbying, and bitterly resists the kind of positive, forward-looking reforms that would put more money and power in the hands of the American people, to whom it belongs in the first place.

But imagine if we decided as a society to go into the new century with a new relationship between "we the people" and "they the government." Imagine if we said "no" to the business-as-usual approach of establishment politicians, high-priced lobbyists, and Washington insiders.

What if we decided to change the rules? To start fresh?

What if:

- Americans had the freedom to participate in this New Economy and raise their families without the fear of being left behind?
- Americans were set free from the fear of the IRS—and free to choose a new tax system that's so honest that we wouldn't need sixty-seven thousand lobbyists in Washington, so simple that people could fill out their taxes on a postcard, and so fair that twenty million low-income Americans would be taken off the tax rolls altogether and an average family of four earning $36,000 would pay no federal income tax at all, a savings of more than $1,600 a year?
- parents were free to choose schools that really work for their children—schools that are safe, clean, disciplined, drug-free, and academically challenging, and that reinforce rather than undermine the moral and spiritual values being taught at home?
- every teacher were free to create such schools, without politicians and bureaucrats draining away badly needed classroom funding and micromanaging their curriculum, not to mention their every move?
- all Americans were free to own their own low-cost catastrophic health insurance policies and Medical Savings Accounts that would give them real peace of mind and the freedom to choose doctors they trust, specialists they need, and second opinions they want for themselves and their families, rather than being forced into top-down, government-run health care programs or heavy-handed HMOs?
- every senior citizen were free from the fear that the Washington politicians were constantly raiding the Social Security Trust Fund to waste it on more big government programs?
- younger workers were free to choose to invest part—and eventually the bulk—of their Social Security taxes in personal

retirement accounts they owned themselves, out of the hands
of the Washington politicians?

- every American were free from the fear of random, violent
  crime—confident that our criminal justice system was not letting dangerous felons out of prison to rob, rape, and kill again?
- every parent and teacher, religious, business, and community
  leader, as well as every sports and entertainment star and
  elected official engaged in a national campaign to help young
  people rediscover a sense of enduring values and be set free
  from the epidemics of teen pregnancy, drug abuse, violence,
  and gang involvement?
- every American were free to enjoy the natural heritage of
  America's air, land, water, and wildlife without the fear of
  increased pollution and decreased property rights?
- every American were free from the fear of ballistic missile
  attacks, international terrorism, and the proliferation of
  nuclear, chemical, and biological weapons of mass destruction?
- every child had the freedom to be born, grow up securely, and
  live peacefully until natural death?

What a different society that would be. America would shine
forth once again as the "city on a hill" that John Winthrop held forth
to our pilgrim forefathers, a light and inspiration to the world. Government of the people, by the people, and for the people would not
perish, but would flourish and thrive for generations to
come. Is it possible to achieve? With all my heart, I believe the
answer is yes. But nothing of great and lasting worth comes easily or
cheaply. As President Teddy Roosevelt once declared: "We shall
never be successful over the dangers that confront us; we shall never
achieve true greatness, nor reach the lofty ideal which the founders
and preservers of our mighty Federal Republic have set before us,
unless we are Americans in heart and soul, in spirit and purpose, keenly alive to the responsibility implied by the very name
American…."

We, the American people, have it in our power to make the world new again. Let us seize the day and win for America its rightful place in the twenty-first century. May generations yet unborn look back and say that the turn of the century marked the dawn of a new era of freedom for America and all mankind.

CHAPTER TWO

THE FREEDOM REVOLUTION

IF YOU ASK Milton Friedman, the wonderfully insightful Nobel Prize–winning economist, about the state of American freedom, he will likely tell you the parable of the frog and the kettle. If you put a frog in a kettle of boiling hot water, it will jump out immediately. But if you put a frog in a kettle of cold water and slowly turn up the heat, the frog will stay put, and eventually boil to death. Today, slowly but surely, our freedoms are being taken away from us. But because they aren't being taken away all at once, it is easy not to notice. If we are not careful, says Dr. Friedman, we may someday realize to our horror that we all have been cooked. He's right.

Would you sit still if the Washington politicians decreed that Social Security tax rates should be six times higher? It's already happened. Over the past fifty years, the rate has climbed from 2 percent to 12.4 percent.

Would you sit still while a foreign enemy wiped out 40 percent of our army, half of our air force, and 40 percent of our navy? Don't worry. The current administration has already done it through budget cuts.

Would you sit still while the percentage of American teenagers using heroin doubled in a single decade? It's already happened.

Since 1990, use of this dangerous and destructive drug by young people has skyrocketed and purity has increased dramatically, while the average price on the street has dropped by nearly two-thirds.

This is not freedom. It is social suicide. We cannot sit idly by and watch our financial security, national defenses, and children's safety be taken away from us. It's time to fight back.

Would you sit still if Washington politicians decreed that Social Security tax rates should be six times higher? It's already happened. Over the past fifty years, the rate has climbed from 2 percent to 12.4 percent.

But if we have already lost so much ground, is it really possible to turn things around and experience a new birth of freedom?

The answer is yes. The reasons derive from three great events that are already transforming our society—the end of the Cold War, the dawn of the Information Age, and encouraging signs of another moral and spiritual awakening.

THE END OF THE COLD WAR

We take the end of the Cold War for granted, but it has enormous implications for our system of self-government. To understand why, just ask yourself: How did America—the most pro-individual, anti-statist nation ever invented—come to permit its government to assume the size and scope that it has today? The root cause is war—the great shaper of this century. Throughout history, warfare fostered government centralization. You cannot face a major external threat unless you have a strong government to marshal the resources necessary to meet that threat. For most of the past eighty years, America has faced a major external threat of one sort or another—first World War I, then World War II, and finally the Cold War.

These conflicts have been cited to justify government expansion in every direction. How did we justify federal aid to education? The initial rationale was national security, the idea that more funding would make better schools which would make smarter students which would help us defeat the Soviets. Federal aid for research and development and the space program? National security. Even the interstate highway program begun in the 1950s was partially justified on national security grounds. It seemed natural to some that if government could mobilize resources to fight external enemies, it could solve an array of domestic problems as well; hence, the "War on Poverty."

It has taken us a long time to learn, very painfully, the limitations of big government. Now that the Cold War is over, we no longer need such a massive, centralized federal government. We now have the opportunity to downsize Washington and shift money, power, and control back to individuals, families, and local communities. Just as Teddy Roosevelt started the new century by attacking government corruption at its source and busting up anti-competitive monopolies, it is time to start the next century by shrinking big government. That means junking the current federal income tax code—the biggest source of political pollution and corruption in this country—and replacing it with a simple, honest, and fair flat tax that also lowers everyone's tax bill. That means creating a new Social Security system of personal retirement accounts for younger workers, expanding Medical Savings Accounts for working families and seniors on Medicare, and expanding parental control over where their children go to school and what values they are being taught. After all, it is the moral right of parents—not government—to decide what is best for their children.

The end of the Cold War also means that people all around the world are discovering, some for the very first time, what free markets and free elections are all about. It means Americans now have the opportunity to sell our goods and services in markets long closed to us. It means we can find new partners in the never-ending battle against terrorism and tyranny. Now is not the time for America to turn inward and abandon our role as leader of a potentially expanding free world. Instead, we must show the world how a free people can rediscover their first principles amidst changing times and circumstances.

THE DAWN OF A NEW INFORMATION AGE

At the same time, it is almost impossible to overstate the changes our society is going through as we make the difficult but critical transition from the Machine Age to the Microchip Age.

The Machine Age was all about bigness—big factories, big companies, big unions, big cities, and, of course, big government. It was a direct byproduct of the spirit of American enterprise. Led by the Fords, the Rockefellers, the Morgans, and the Carnegies, America was in the forefront in making cars, steel, ships, trains, tanks, airplanes—you name it, Americans built it. Millions of people have grown up under the rules of the Machine Age. And they were good rules, rules that worked, rules people understood. You could graduate from high school, get a job at the local plant, join the union, make a good wage, buy a home, raise a family. There was job security and close friends and neighbors you went to work with. It wasn't easy, but it was a good life. It was real, and it was safe.

Now the rules are changing—and they're changing fast.

Today we are at the dawn of a new Information Age economic era—symbolized by the microchip—which is transforming the way we live and the way we work. The microchip is extending the reach of the human brain the way machines extended the reach of human muscle starting two hundred years ago. Think about it. Learn to drive a tractor and you could do more work in a day than a hundred Herculean plowmen could do in a month in days of old. But now, learn to use a personal computer and you can produce more work from an office or your den in a few hours than someone with an entire secretarial and research staff could produce in a week just twenty or thirty years ago.

This New Economy is also a direct byproduct of the spirit of American enterprise, and it's all happening at blinding speeds.

When I graduated from college in 1970, for example, the Intel Corporation—one of the great pioneers of the microchip—was only two years old. Microsoft wasn't even born yet. Nor was Apple, or Oracle, or Compaq, or Sun Microsystems, or Netscape, or Yahoo!, or Amazon.Com, or eBay. Yet by 1997 microchip maker Intel had become the nation's fifth wealthiest company, with a market value bigger than Chrysler, General Motors, and Ford, *combined*.

Just to put it in perspective, when *Forbes* magazine was founded in 1917, steelmakers reigned supreme. The U.S. Steel Company was the mother of all manufacturers, with three times more assets than the next largest company. Their total assets in today's dollars were about $31 billion—blast furnaces, rolling mills, barges, coal mines, ships, shipyards, and 268,000 employees churning out twenty-three million tons of metal each and every year. Today, not a single steel company makes it on the list of the top one hundred American companies. The U.S. Steel Company—now known as USX—employs less than 21,000 employees, down 90 percent from its glory days.

At the same time, computer technology has exploded into the world marketplace. Just look at what has happened. A computer once filled an entire room; today it fits in your pocket. One of the first computers—the Eniac—was incredibly slow. The joke at the time was that the Eniac "could make a twenty-four–hour weather forecast in twenty-five hours." Now a single microchip can perform a billion calculations in the blink of an eye. Once, "debugging" a computer literally meant finding and extricating a moth from a computer known as the Mark II. Today, it means solving the Year 2000 computer problem before the bridge to the twenty-first century gets shut down indefinitely. Bell Labs invented the transistor in 1947. Today, a single Intel Pentium III microchip has the power of 9.5 million transistors. In 1949 Claude Shannon built the first chess-playing computer in the world. In 1997, IBM's Deep Blue supercomputer actually defeated Garry Kasparov, the world's best chess player. A half-century ago, business leaders thought there wouldn't be much of a market for computers. Today, technology is transforming American life.

Perhaps Arthur Clarke, author of *2001: A Space Odyssey*, put it best when he said, "Any sufficiently advanced technology is indistinguishable from magic." How true. We can speak into a little piece of plastic called a cellular phone and talk to anyone, anywhere from any place at any time. We can now see three dimensional images of our children's heart and fingers before they are born, still inside their mother's womb, on a screen in a doctor's office. We can monitor the movements of our enemies from space, and even take a photograph of a terrorist's license plate from a spy satellite thousands of miles up above. George Gilder, one of the prophets and philosophers of modern technology, talks about the marvels of fiber-optic lines that transmit audio, video, and data at the speed of light through "a thread as thin as a human hair, as long as Long Island, fed by a laser that's bright as the sun." OK, so our government still has trouble delivering the mail on time. But the Microchip Age is addressing that too: Now we have fax machines, e-mail, and the Internet to help us (not to mention private package delivery companies like Federal Express and United Parcel Service that use state-of-the-art information technology systems to track our package's every movement).

While the Machine Age was all about bigness, the Microchip Age is almost Jeffersonian in its dynamic—anti-hierarchical, anti-authoritarian, anti-centralization. Suddenly power is shifting out of the hands of government bureaucrats and corporate chieftains, and into the hands of entrepreneurs, employees, and individual customers.

Some people fear that in this new era if they aren't up to speed on programming, or aren't some kind of high-tech jockey, they are going to be left behind. Not true. One of the virtues of a free society is that you succeed most when you offer a product or service that people find simple and easy to use. For example, you don't need to be an engineer to buy and drive an automobile. You don't need to know anything about aerodynamics to buy an airplane ticket and travel around the country or the world. So, too, you don't need to know anything about "m–ps" or "b–ps" or "l–ps" or "bytes" or whatever high-tech jargon is floating out there to be able to participate in this new era.

Just look at one of the early fruits of the Information Age: the calculator. Thirty years ago a calculator cost over $1,000. Today the packaging costs more than the gizmo itself. Everyone has one now, and they are simple and easy to use. Even people who never felt comfortable doing math in school can, with a calculator, do in a matter of seconds or minutes the type of mathematical computations it would have taken math whizzes hours or days to do just forty or fifty years ago. Now we think it's the most natural thing in the world, and this is just an example of what lies ahead.

In the Microchip Age, a single mom can put her kids in bed at eight or nine o'clock at night, log onto the Internet, balance her checkbook, glance at the news headlines she was too busy to watch on television, check tomorrow's weather forecast, and send an e-mail message to her sister halfway across the country or halfway around the world.

A retired couple can create a used book business and run it right out of their own home. For modest start-up costs, they can buy a personal computer, create a website, send out bulk e-mails, take on-line orders, take on-line credit card numbers, search for hard-to-find books through sophisticated computerized databases, and track their Fed-Ex shipping accounts, all without renting a store front, hiring a staff, or carrying a huge overhead.

A high school student doing a research paper on new advances in fighting cancer can access the world's great libraries and health organizations through the World Wide Web, correspond with medical researchers via e-mail, and transmit her finished report to her teacher electronically, all from the safety and comfort of her own home.

That's what the Microchip Age is all about—putting power and control back in the hands of people who once felt they were mere cogs in the corporate wheel.

It's exciting. But it's also a very different world from what most people are used to. The rules of the Microchip Age are not the same as the Machine Age. And this is something to which the political culture in Washington seems oblivious. For example, to help people compete and succeed in the Microchip Age, we can't allow our senior high school students to finish nineteenth in math and sixteenth in science out of twenty-one countries taking international tests. Not everyone has to go to college. Bill Gates and Rush Limbaugh never finished college, and they have done pretty well for themselves. But it does put an enormous burden on K-12 education to do the job right. Otherwise, kids are going to be left behind, trapped in jobs that can't possibly pay for the kind of life they want and deserve.

This new era also requires giving people the freedom to set up a business in a spare bedroom, or garage, or small office, without having to comply with a blizzard of government rules and regulations and punishing, sky-high taxes (like taxes on Internet commerce) that can smother the enthusiasm of all but the most determined new entrepreneurs. Nor can we focus on only small and start-up companies. We also must remove the tax and regulatory burdens that threaten to hinder the long-term success of larger American companies that are now operating in a rapidly changing and highly competitive global marketplace. And we must be extremely aggressive in busting open new markets for American goods and services, not roll over and play dead when foreign countries tell us we are not welcome. This is absolutely critical to staying on economic offense as we go into the twenty-first century. If we fail to make these and other fundamental reforms, American companies will look elsewhere and move their operations to countries that do create a more hospitable business environment. That, in turn, will destroy American jobs, harm our competitiveness, and hinder our economic growth—precisely what we do not want to do.

FREEDOM WITH RESPONSIBILITY: A NEW GREAT AWAKENING

The third great change that is transforming our society in addition to the end of the Cold War and the rise of the microchip is evidence that we may be in the early stages of a new moral and spiritual awakening. In my chapter on "The Moral Basis of a Free Society," I describe this in some detail. But it is important to note here that something positive and counterintuitive is under way in our country, even if the mainstream media hasn't quite caught up with it yet.

One by one, day by day, we as Americans are beginning to wake up, as from a deep sleep. We are beginning to realize that a self-governing nation must be made up of self-governing individuals. We are beginning to confront the sad and bitter reality that something has gone terribly wrong in our culture since the 1960s, that the enduring values upon which we built this great country have faded from view. Somewhere along the way, we started letting young people think that freedom was some sort of a license to do your own thing and make up the rules along the way. "If it feels good, do it" became the slogan of an entire generation. Now we are suffering the whirlwind.

Over the past several years, I have traveled to all fifty states, and wherever I go I meet parents and pastors, teachers and young people who echo a common refrain: "This isn't supposed to happen here." Sometimes they're talking about what they see on the evening news—the horror of violence on our city streets and in our suburban neighborhoods. Sometimes they're talking about what they hear on the radio—people calling into Dr. Laura Schlessinger's program to talk about the immense personal pain that they hold just under the surface of their lives—the pain of separation, divorce, loneliness, problems with their children, and abuse. Sometimes they're talking about the garbage that's on daytime TV, or in the movies, or in the music their kids listen to, or available on the Internet. Sometimes they're talking about what they are hearing from the guidance counselors in schools, how the epidemic of fatherlessness in America is hollowing out our kids emotionally and intellectually and causing an explosion in teen drug abuse, suicide, and juvenile violent crime.

It happened again in Littleton, Colorado. The midday massacre in Columbine High School stopped America's emotional traffic dead in its tracks. In a flash of gunfire and homemade bombs, we found ourselves forced to stare into the heart of darkness. In the faces of grieving parents, children, and teachers we were forced to confront the sobering reality that all is not well in our country just because the Dow Jones Industrial Average is riding high. As a nation, we may be materially better off than we were a generation ago, but clearly we are raising a generation in which too many young people are spiritually impoverished, without a sense of right and wrong.

My wife and I were horrified when we learned what had happened in Littleton. As we thought about and prayed for the families and friends of the dead and wounded, I just kept thinking about when our five girls were born. They were magic times, times of innocence and sweetness. But like every parent, I knew tough times lay ahead. It is then that you realize what parenting is really all about, helping children establish a moral compass, a sense of purpose and direction based on transcendent truths that will last them for a lifetime through the good times and the bad.

Young people in every generation are searching for security and significance. Our times are no exception. Kids want to love and be loved. They want to know and be known. They are wired to be dreamers. They have a vivid imagination and are hungry to be part of something larger than themselves. They want to change the world, and they long for heroes who will show them the way.

But nature abhors a vacuum. Children who grow up without

fathers will seek out father figures, even those that may cause them harm. Children who grow up without love will learn to hate. Children who grow up spiritually empty—adrift in a culture of alienation and violence without an anchor for their souls—are vulnerable to the seductions of evil. Littleton reminded us of these cold, hard truths, as if the school shootings in Paducah, Kentucky, and Jonesboro, Arkansas, the bombing in Oklahoma City, and the horrifying dragging death of a black man in Jasper, Texas, were not enough.

Clearly we are raising a generation of young people who are spiritually impoverished, without a sense of right and wrong.

Some look at all the evidence and see a glass half empty. They see America going to hell in a handbasket, without hope. I understand that view, but I don't share it. I believe that such moments of personal and national terror and pain are forcing each of us to reconsider our own values, our own spiritual beliefs, and our own approach to raising our children. The sheer magnitude of our cultural disease is beginning to create its own antibodies. More and more people are saying, "Enough is enough," and they are looking for real solutions to the problems we face. Why is Oprah Winfrey speaking out against trash TV and using her show to talk about the deeper things of life? Why is Dr. Laura an overnight radio success story? Why are baby boomers and their children returning to church and synagogue by the millions? Why have so many men participated in the Promise Keepers rallies? Why was Bill Bennett's 800-plus-page *Book of Virtues* a *New York Times* best-seller? Why have North Carolina author Jan Karon's books about a kindly Episcopal priest and a gentle little town called Mitford become runaway hits, selling more than three million copies over the past five years alone? Why has such an uplifting and spiritual television program as *Touched By An Angel* become so popular? Why are federal and state governments passing "welfare-to-work" and "three-strikes-and-you're-out" laws and achieving dramatic reductions in welfare dependency and violent crime? Why are elected officials beginning to look for help for the poor and disadvantaged from private, faith-based schools and charities? Why has a national conversation about our children and our values once again become acceptable in the public square after decades of derision and controversy? To me, the answer is obvious. One by one, day by day, Americans are starting to fight back for the freedom to do justice, love mercy, and walk humbly with their God. This is why I have hope for the future.

GREAT STRUGGLES FOR FREEDOM

Another reason for my optimism is that we as Americans have suc-cessfully gone through several great struggles to expand individual freedom and equal justice since John Hancock put his John Han-cock on the Declaration of Independence on July 4, 1776.

With the signing of the Emancipation Proclamation on January 1, 1863, amidst an ongoing Civil War between North and South, President Abraham Lincoln officially moved to right a ter-rible wrong, declaring that several million black men, women, and children "shall be then, thenceforward, and forever free."

It was the beginning of a long and bloody road to civil rights and personal freedom, a road that would lead through Gettysburg, Pennsylvania, during the summer of 1863. Thousands of soldiers, from both sides, lay dead. The Union had successfully repelled a Confederate attack, which many believe was the turning point of the war. On November 19, 1863, President Lincoln attended a special ceremony honoring those who had fallen. Edward Everett, a well-known orator, gave an address that lasted almost two hours. Lincoln spoke for little more than two minutes. Everett would later send a note to the president, saying: *"Permit me... to express my great admiration for the thoughts expressed by you, with such eloquent sim-plicity and appropriateness, at the consecration of the cemetery. I should be glad, if I could flatter myself, that I came as near to the central idea of the occasion in two hours, as you did in two minutes."*

Though Lincoln himself would not live to see the struggle through, at Gettysburg he had indeed captured the "central idea" of the American experiment in freedom. For it was there, "met on a great battlefield of that war," that Lincoln spoke of "a new birth of freedom."

> Fourscore and seven years ago our fathers brought forth on this continent a new nation, conceived in liberty, and dedicated to the proposition that all men are created equal…. The world will little note nor long remember what we say here, but it can never forget what they did here. It is for us, the living, rather, to be dedicated here to the unfinished work which they who fought here have thus far so nobly advanced. It is rather for us to be here dedicated to the great task remaining before us—that from these honored dead we take increased devotion to that cause for which they gave the last full measure of devotion; that we here highly resolve that these dead shall not have died in vain; that this nation, under God, shall have a new birth of freedom; and that government of the people, by the people, for the people, shall not perish from the earth.

By the early years of the twentieth century, just about the time my grandfather came to this country, Americans were once again filled with optimism about the future of freedom. The nation's rapid industrialization and urbanization created enormous new social, economic, and political problems, but these were confronted by bold, imaginative national leaders and the energetic efforts of people voluntarily working together to promote shared objectives.

America did not glide painlessly into the twentieth century. The years leading up to it were a troubled time. The rise of large corporations and massive industrial monopolies seemed to mock the idea of individual entrepreneurship. The rise of big cities with corrupt political machines supplanted the tradition of democratic town meetings. People feared that massive immigration, which was several times greater in proportion than what we are experiencing today, would degrade the American character and culture. How, they asked, could we assimilate so many people from so many different races, nationalities, and religions? These years were also plagued by drug addiction—primarily to opium.

American churches and synagogues responded to the challenge of the new industrial era by combining a message of spiritual renewal with practical, personal care for those in need. Dwight L. Moody, a former shoe salesman, became the most influential American evangelist of the nineteenth century. He launched a Sunday School movement in Chicago to provide moral instruction for more than fifteen hundred poor, urban street children. He opened a Bible college to challenge other young people to follow his example of helping destitute and demoralized people turn their lives around. And, in an age without radio or television, he communicated his message of spiritual and moral renewal to millions of people before his death in 1899.

The spiritual and practical needs of America's burgeoning city populations were also addressed by social reformers such as William and Catherine Booth, who founded the Salvation Army in the United States in 1880. Women took a particular interest in the needs of those who found themselves financially and morally bankrupt. By 1913 more than five hundred urban rescue missions were operating in the United States and Canada, many of them organized and run by women of faith. Catholic nuns and Jewish and other fraternal societies also labored to help the needy everywhere, from little mining towns to urban slums.

At the same time, President Theodore Roosevelt was ushering in an era of political and economic reform. He declared in his inaugural address: "Much has been given us, and much will rightfully be expected from us. Our forefathers faced certain perils which we have outgrown. We now face other perils, the very existence of which it was impossible that they should foresee. Modern life is both complex and intense, and the tremendous changes wrought by the extraordinary industrial development of the last half-century are felt in every fiber of our social and political being."

From 1901 to 1909 Roosevelt sought to expand individual opportunity and strengthen individual control over personal, business, and political affairs, as well as increase America's economic and military influence in the world. He busted up incestuous and anti-competitive trusts and corporate monopolies; attacked government and political corruption in both major parties; supported the right of workers to organize; expanded U.S. trade with other nations; and built up our armed forces, particularly the navy. He advocated the direct election of U.S. senators, the right of women to vote, the creation of open presidential primaries, and the introduction of citizen initiatives, referenda, and recalls—all of which would soon become realities.

Roosevelt reinforced his battle for political and economic reform by publicly, vigorously, and consistently reasserting the notion that there must be a moral foundation to a free society. It was he, after all, who coined the term "bully pulpit." While governor of New York, Roosevelt once declared, "It is absolutely impossible for a Republic long to endure if it becomes either corrupt or cowardly"—and he never lost sight of that essential truth. He rightly believed that private, local, character-forming institutions must be left free to strengthen the moral fiber of the nation. The role of religious faith in society must be affirmed, not undermined. He did not believe that government should establish a state religion. But he did not shrink from the right or responsibility of a public official to encourage individuals to attend to their moral and spiritual character.

Not all of Roosevelt's policies were wise (he vigorously argued for a graduated income tax, for example). Some of his policies, such as trust busting, made particular sense for his time, but should be adapted in our day to such causes as breaking up government education and entitlement monopolies in favor of individual and parental choice and control. Still, Roosevelt lived during a period of historic change from the Age of Agriculture to the Age of Industry; his vigorous spirit of renewal and reform on behalf of individuals and families should inspire us today as we make the transition from the Age of Industry to the Age of Information.

By the 1960s the civil rights movement for individual freedom and equal justice under the law was reaching its zenith. It was a painful, turbulent time. But the moral imperative of the cause was captured eloquently by Dr. Martin Luther King, Jr., in a speech he delivered on the steps of the Lincoln Memorial on August 28, 1963. The "I Have a Dream" speech came to symbolize the movement. By 1964 the Civil Rights Act was passed by Congress and signed by the president.

"Fivescore years ago, a great American, in whose symbolic shadow we stand, signed the Emancipation Proclamation," Dr. King began, noting that "one hundred years later, we must face the tragic fact that the Negro is still not free.... One hundred years later, the Negro lives on a lonely island of poverty in the midst of a vast ocean of material prosperity."

He went on to say that he refused to believe that "the bank of justice is bankrupt." He refused to believe that there are "insufficient funds in the great vaults of opportunity of this nation," adding that "now is the time to open the doors of opportunity to all of God's children."

On that remarkable August day, Dr. King shared his dream of America with America, a dream of equal opportunity, justice, and freedom:

> I say to you today, my friends, that in spite of the difficulties and frustrations of the moment I still have a dream. It is a dream deeply rooted in the American dream.... I have a dream that my four little children will one day live in a nation where they will not be judged

by the color of their skin but by the content of their character.

It is a dream we must press on to fulfill as we head into the twenty-first century.

By the late 1970s a great struggle for freedom was needed once again. At home, we faced the most serious economic crisis since the Great Depression. Abroad, the Soviet empire was on the offensive, American prestige and credibility were in doubt, and freedom was in retreat. Into the breach stepped Ronald Reagan.

Reagan shared Abraham Lincoln's deep-rooted belief that all men are created equal and have the unalienable right to life, liberty, and the pursuit of happiness. He shared Teddy Roosevelt's love of a strong military and the great outdoors. He also shared Dr. King's ability to drive his message of freedom deep into the human heart.

Perhaps even more important, Ronald Reagan understood the times and knew what America should do. To restore the economic security and prosperity of the American people, he slashed federal income taxes by 25 percent across the board, simplified the tax code by reducing the number of tax rates to just two, busted open new foreign markets to U.S. goods and services, dramatically reduced suffocating regulations on American businesses, and pursued sound monetary policies to stop the ravages of inflation. To protect the security of the American people, Reagan rebuilt our military that had been hollowed out so badly during the 1970s; began developing a ballistic missile defense system; reinvigorated American alliances in Europe, Asia, Latin America, and Israel; and challenged Soviet adventurism wherever communism reared its ugly head. And his strategy worked.

> **We have launched freedom revolutions before in our history.... I believe we can do so again.**

In his nationally televised farewell address on January 11, 1989, President Reagan shared his thoughts on eight years on the front lines of freedom. A few lines have always stayed with me:

> Ours was the first revolution in the history of mankind that truly reversed the course of government, and with three little words: We the People. We the People tell the government what to do; it doesn't tell us. We the People are the driver; the government is the car. And we decide where it should go, and by what route, and how fast. Almost all the world's constitutions are documents in which governments tell the people what their privileges are. Our Constitution is a document in which We the People tell the government what it is allowed to do. We the People are free. This belief has been the underlying basis for everything I've tried to do these past eight years.

It has been a decade since Ronald Reagan left Washington. The Berlin Wall has fallen, the Soviet empire has collapsed, fledgling democracies are springing up all over the world, and our economic expansion is now nearly two decades old, fueled by a technological revolution that still mystifies and amazes.

Yes, we now face a new century with serious new challenges, and yes, we have experienced a decade of political drift and disappointment. But we have launched freedom revolutions before in our history, and met great success. I believe we can do so again.

CHAPTER THREE

THE MAGIC OF
A FREE SOCIETY

THE YEAR WAS 1918. War had engulfed Europe. A revolution was sweeping through Russia. And a little boy was born in a small town in Oklahoma.

His parents believed that in America the sky was the limit. The secret was "work, work, work," his father would say. And his parents certainly practiced what they preached. Whether it was selling real estate and insurance or starting their own dairy business, they worked hard and tried to get ahead. Little did they know that of their two sons, one would grow up to succeed beyond their wildest dreams.

The young boy was Sam Walton, the founder of Wal-Mart.

With a degree in business from the University of Missouri in Columbia, and some experience as a management trainee at a J.C. Penney store in Des Moines, Iowa, Walton borrowed $25,000 from his father-in-law just after getting out of the military after World War II. He bought a Ben Franklin variety store in Newport, Arkansas. By 1985 *Forbes* named him the wealthiest man in America, with a net worth of about $2.8 billion. When he died on April 5, 1992, at the age of seventy-four, his assets were worth almost ten times that amount, and Wal-Mart had surpassed Sears as the largest retailer in America.

How did he do it? Some call it greed. But it wasn't. My brother, Tim, captured it perfectly in his foreword to *Forbes' Greatest Business Stories Of All Time*: "Wal-Mart gave rural Americans, people of modest means, more choice and quality for less cost. Its founder, Sam Walton, became the richest man in the world… by stretching other people's scarce and hard-earned dollars further. He improved on the margin the quality of life for millions of people. That is his real legacy, and it points to the ethical heart of business: service to others. Without it, no enterprise and no entrepreneur can succeed."

Walton understood the promise of the Microchip Age. His stores were the first discount retailer to test the UPC price scanning system in 1980. It increased productivity by 50 percent and soon became standard in every store. With new computer technology, Walton sought to keep his stores on the cutting edge—ahead of his competition—tracking sales, inventories, payroll, and marketing trends, and even communicating with his nearly two thousand stores via his own Hughes Network Systems six-channel satellite. From his high-tech, computerized command post (built in 1984 in Bentonville, Arkansas, the building is larger than a football field), Walton and his associates could look for inefficiencies in every area of a store's operations.

But to Sam Walton, technology was a means, not an end. His state-of-the-art monitoring system was no substitute for the instincts of good managers and employees on the ground. His goal was to serve his customers the best that he could. He worked with suppliers to help them become more efficient, knowing that if his suppliers cut their costs, he could cut his, and his customers could enjoy lower prices. He encouraged store managers and employees to come up with innovative new ideas to save money and improve service.

"Try anyone's idea," Walton would say. "It might not work. But it won't break the company when it doesn't."

"One of Sam's greatest contributions to Wal-Mart," said one of his suppliers, "was his attitude toward experimentation. He constantly encouraged us to experiment on a small basis and if the idea worked, roll it out. If it failed, try something else. It was his attitude of keep trying, and don't be afraid of failure."

Walton himself believed that this spirit of innovation—out of a concern for the customer—was the secret to his success.

"I didn't start as a banker or an investor or doing anything else [other] than waiting on customers," he once wrote in *Wal-Mart-World*, the employee magazine. "Many people who run big companies never ring cash registers, nor do they wait on customers, and so I've always appreciated what it meant to be a salesclerk and how much a salesperson can influence a customer in a business relationship."

The same month that Sam Walton passed away, April of 1992, *The Harvard Business Review* ran an article by three management consultants assessing Wal-Mart's secret of success.

"The job of senior management at Wal-Mart," they wrote, "is not to tell individual store managers what to do but to create an environment where they can learn from the market—and from each other."

Walton gave generously to charities and created a profit-sharing plan that allowed even low-wage employees of his company to retire with generous pensions due to the rapidly rising value of Wal-Mart stock. In fact, perhaps more than anything else, I think he would have liked to read one particular paragraph from his *New York Times* obituary. It told of a Wal-Mart cashier, Shirley Cox, who retired in 1989. On her last day, she earned $7.10 an hour. But in her retirement account was a pension worth $262,000.

This is part of the greatness of America: a young boy growing up during the Depression with good parents who teach him hard work and the value of a dollar, with the freedom to build a business, with the courage to make a difference, becoming the wealthiest man in the world… and a young girl who grows up to work hard and loyally for a strong American company and retire with dignity and security because she was free to participate in the real American economy. In an environment of freedom, real human progress is possible. The least can become first. The establishment can be challenged and the world made anew. This is the magic of a free society.

THE SPIRIT OF ENTERPRISE

Consider the story of Ray Kroc, a milkshake salesman, working hard and trying to get ahead. One day in 1954 he visited a hamburger stand in San Bernadino, California, that would change his life. With burgers for fifteen cents, fries for ten cents, and orders delivered in sixty seconds, the stand was so successful that Maurice and Richard McDonald didn't buy one or two milkshake machines from Kroc; they bought eight. A lightbulb went off. Kroc figured if he could get the McDonald brothers to open more stores, he could sell more milkshake machines. Just one problem: they said no. Kroc knew his own company was under enormous competitive pressure and might soon go under. At fifty-two years old, with thirty years in the sales business, Kroc didn't know what he would do if he lost his job. So Kroc made the McDonald brothers an offer they couldn't refuse: he would do the work—sell the franchises, develop an assembly-line production system, establish a national marketing strategy, and carefully monitor quality in all the new stores—and the brothers would get to keep a small share of the profits. The rest was history. Shortly after Ray Kroc passed away in 1984 at the age of eighty-one, McDonald's sold its fifty-billionth hamburger.

It is this spirit of enterprise—this spirit of risk-taking—that created the American nation and drew people from all over the planet. Most of our families came to these shores escaping tyranny, poverty, religious persecution, and political harassment of one kind or another. Our parents and grandparents desperately wanted to be free to raise their families, run their businesses, and build warm and caring communities where they could be safe, where they could be secure, where they could make a better life for themselves and their children.

America was founded by people who got their human nature right. They understood that the essence of enterprise is the magic and mystery inside the human spirit. It is about the undeniable truth that each of us and all of us have been created in the image of God, and so we are, by nature, creative ourselves. A nation that creates an environment of freedom is a nation that allows people to pursue their dreams, a nation that will succeed beyond its wildest imagination.

The Soviet Union and its communist satellite countries, by contrast, were founded by people who got their human nature wrong. Communism tries to deny that men and women are moral and spiritual beings, endowed by the Creator with certain unalienable rights. Nations that try to crush and imprison the human spirit are doomed to social and financial ruin.

Roberto Goizueta understood this first hand. When he fled Havana, Cuba, in 1961, all he had with him was his wife, kids, and not much more than the clothes on their backs. He had worked for Coca-Cola in Cuba and was able to get a job with Coca-Cola in Miami. But now, in America, he was free to work hard, impress his employers, and rise through the company—and that's precisely what he did. By 1981 Goizueta had become the chief executive officer of the Atlanta-based soda giant. During his tenure, he launched Diet Coke, moved aggressively into foreign markets, launched New Coke (oops!), and always learned from his mistakes to make the company stronger. Under his leadership, the value of Coke stock rose 3,900 percent. Roberto Goizueta came to America with twenty dollars in his pocket. When he passed away in 1997, he was one of America's most successful businessmen.

Andy Grove escaped communist Hungary in 1956—and communism's loss was freedom's gain. For in an environment of freedom, Grove was able to discover and develop his God-given talents, dramatically advance the development of the microchip, and, in the process, become one of the fathers of the Information Age. He built Intel into the world's largest microchip maker and one of the most successful companies in America.

Individual freedom and equal opportunity are not just the answers to bettering the lives of those oppressed by communism in foreign lands, however. They are also balms that can help heal the wounds and right the wrongs of slavery and racial injustice here in America.

"I have a dream that one day even the state of Mississippi, a desert state sweltering with the heat of injustice and oppression, will be transformed into an oasis of freedom and justice," declared Dr. Martin Luther King, Jr., on the steps of the Lincoln Memorial in 1963. Slowly but surely, his dream is coming true.

DREAMS REALLY CAN COME TRUE

Consider Oprah Winfrey. She was born in rural Mississippi, became a newscaster in Nashville, moved to Chicago, took a third-rated morning television show to the top and then syndicated it nationally. *Oprah* is now one of the highest rated daytime television talk shows in America, a country whose black population is about 12 percent.

Along the way, Oprah has become an intriguing missionary for the gospel of free enterprise. A few years ago, she renounced the typical daytime TV fare of wallowing in the stories of freaks. Now she encourages viewers to start their own businesses, showcases success stories, runs her own book club to promote reading and personal growth, and has devoted her 1998–1999 broadcasting season to what she calls "Change Your Life TV."

Any way you slice it, Oprah Winfrey is living the American dream—doing what she was born to do—and rightfully reaping the rewards. In the process, she's inspiring others to achieve their dreams and tap the enormous potential within them. She is making the case by what she says and how she lives that wealth is good and in America dreams really can come true.

FREE MINDS AND FREE MARKETS

It is all part of a remarkable paradigm shift under way in American society and around the world—a triumph of trust in free minds and free markets over a dependence on centrally planned, top-down, government-run societies. In the 1980s wealth and free enterprise were widely derided in the media as evil, much as the military was once derided during the peak years of the Vietnam War. Typical were cutthroat businessmen like Gordon Gekko in the movie *Wall Street*, who said things like "Greed is good" and then played terrible games with people's lives.

Today, however, the cultural tide is turning. The New Economy has emerged. Entrepreneurship is in. A new generation of investors is on the rise. Stephen Covey's *The Seven Habits of Highly Effective People*, published in 1989, is now an international best-seller, with more than fourteen million copies in print. Books on financial freedom and creating small businesses have raced to the top of the best-seller lists. More than 125 million Americans are now invested in the stock market, and 401(k) plans and Individual Retirement Accounts are more popular than ever before. The *Wall Street Journal* is the nation's most widely read newspaper. New business magazines—such as *WorkingWoman, Black Enterprise,* and *Entrepreneur*—have exploded onto the scene in the past several decades. Business-oriented cable television networks—such as CNBC, CNNfn, MSNBC, and the Fox News Channel—are themselves becoming big business. On-line investing is surging in popularity. And from movies like *Forrest Gump* (in which the lead character, played by Tom Hanks, starts his own businesses and goes from rags to riches with a good heart and a giving spirit) to *Jerry Maguire* (in which a sports agent played by Tom Cruise starts his own successful business after losing his job with a big, prestigious firm), even Hollywood cannot completely seem to resist the *zeitgeist* of this exciting Age of Opportunity.

With the fall of the Berlin Wall, the dawn of the Information Age, and generally good economic times throughout much of the

United States, most Americans (outside of college professors) now believe that Ronald Reagan was right when he said that America's free market system was good and moral, while the Soviet Union's totalitarian system made it an "evil empire." Just look at the steady hum of commerce occurring in this "city on a hill." Americans of all ages, races, and economic backgrounds are going into business for themselves in record numbers. Between 1980 and 1996, for example, the number of sole proprietorships in the United States shot up 72 percent, and the total number of American businesses grew from 13.8 million to over 23 million.

WOMEN IN THE AGE OF OPPORTUNITY

Women have become a driving force in this Age of Opportunity. In 1997 they ran 8.5 million companies—about one-third of all U.S. enterprises—and employed more than 23 million Americans, according to a study by the National Foundation for Women Business Owners. These companies generate more than $3 trillion in revenue, and women are now starting new businesses at twice the rate of men. In fact, between 1987 and 1997 alone, the number of women-owned businesses in the United States shot up 90 percent, while their total sales shot up by 160 percent.

Many of these enterprises are being created by stay-at-home moms. In 1980 a *Forbes* cover story estimated that there were then about 350,000 women-owned, home-based businesses in America. By 1995 there were ten times that number and the trend continues today. According to a May 1998 *Forbes* story entitled "Entrepreneur Moms" by reporter Luisa Kroll, "few things have done more for at-home entrepreneurs than the Internet." Emanuela Bradley, for example, "consoled herself by surfing the Internet" while on bedrest during a complicated pregnancy in 1996. She joined an e-mail network of other stay-at-home moms and met Marla Jennings, a mother of three and the creator of her own gift basket business. The two had a brain storm. Why not create an on-line mall to help other home-based businesses sell their wares? So they teamed up and in September of 1997 launched The At-Home Shop, an on-line mall with "thirty vendors, twenty-five of which are home-based businesses run by women." Nor are they alone. Karen Benton of York, Pennsylvania, told *Forbes* that she earns $100,000 a year from selling handwoven baskets through a home-based business. Several of the great benefits are being your own boss, setting your own pace, and creating your own dress code. "Society has gone through several stages of blue collar and white collar," she says. "Now, it's the open collar." Concluded reporter Kroll: "That's social class that Karl Marx never figured on. But then, he could never have conceived of a society as flexible as ours."

Mary Kay Cosmetics alone has helped over a half million women create their own home-based businesses. In the process, the company has awarded some ten thousand pink Cadillacs and other cars to women who have reached new heights. Launched on Friday, September 13, 1963, by an unemployed mom—Mary Kay Ash—and her twenty-year-old son, the company now does over $1 billion a year in sales in some twenty-seven countries.

> "Society has gone through several stages of blue collar and white collar. Now, it's the open collar."

THE GROWTH
OF BLACK ENTERPRISE

Black Americans are also opening up new businesses in dramatic numbers. In 1995, for example, the U.S. Census Bureau issued a snapshot study showing that the number of black-owned businesses grew 46 percent between 1987 and 1992, with average annual sales of about $52,000. Ninety-four percent of those firms were sole proprietorships. What's more, between 1987 and 1996, the number of black women—owned businesses in the United States increased by 135 percent. New technology—particularly the Internet—is now opening even more doors. "Black-owned businesses must generate new products and services and keep pace with technology to expand their markets and make their businesses more effective," said Dr. Thomas Boston, an economics professor at the Georgia Institute of Technology, in a 1998 interview with *Black Enterprise*. Rick Adams, director of sales operations for e-commerce solutions at IBM, told the *Orlando Sentinel* in May of 1999: "One of the great things about the Internet is it's a great equalizer. It diminishes barriers that minority companies often experience when people see their color."

HISPANICS AND
THE AMERICAN DREAM

Americans of Hispanic descent are now creating new businesses faster than any other ethnic group. Between 1970 and 1990 the number of Hispanic-owned businesses in California exploded by 787 percent. Nationally, between 1987 and 1992 alone, the U.S. Census Bureau found that the number of U.S. Hispanic-owned businesses surged by 76 percent. Hispanic women are also creating their own enterprises at an unprecedented rate—up 206 percent nationally between 1987 and 1996. The U.S. Hispanic Chamber of Commerce now projects that there will be about 2 million Hispanic-owned businesses by the year 2000. There already are some 250 Hispanic Chambers of Commerce across the country. And who won the Chamber's "Hispanic Businesswoman of the Year Award" in 1998? Lavonne Luquis, president and co-founder of *LatinoLink*, the nation's first Hispanic-focused magazine on the World Wide Web. It is all further evidence of the exciting opportunities that lie ahead in this New Economy.

While all this is encouraging, of course, the blunt truth is that there are still far, far too many tax and regulatory obstacles holding back men and women of all races and ethnic groups who want to experience the American dream and go into business for themselves. When I presented a number of Entrepreneur-of-the-Year awards at a Hispanic Business Roundtable luncheon in Washington, D.C., in 1998, Bill Guerrero, the group's president, spoke quite candidly about the massive barriers to entrepreneurship and opportunity that his community still faces. He was particularly interested in the flat tax because the average Hispanic household income is about $35,000 and the flat tax exempts a family of four's first $36,000. That would save millions of families about $1,600 a year. That's real money for real people struggling to move ahead.

Creating personal wealth—not redistributing it—should be one of America's highest priorities as we move into the new century.

This is why I believe so strongly that—despite the naysayers in Washington—now is the time to remove all these artificial obstacles and give all Americans the freedom to create real personal wealth for themselves and their families. In fact, creating personal wealth—not redistributing it—should be one of America's highest priorities as we move into the new century.

WHAT IS WEALTH?

In ages past, when people thought of wealth, they thought of material things—land, armies, jewels, and piles of gold. But as we enter this new Information Age, knowledge-based economy, we are rediscovering an important truth: the real source of wealth and capital in this new era is not material things—it is the human mind, the human spirit, the human imagination, and our faith in the future.

Take oil, for example. When you stop and think about it, oil does not really have value in and of itself. It's just glop. You can't eat it. You can't drink it. You can't even feed it to camels. When oil was first discovered in Pennsylvania in the nineteenth century, it was actually considered a depressor of property values. All this gooey stuff made land impossible to farm. Livestock were getting sick from trying to eat it. So what made it valuable? Human ingenuity. People put their minds to work and invented uses for oil from energy to plastics—and turned this glop into great value.

The same is true of Silicon Valley, one of the wealthiest places in the world because it is the home of some of the world's leading computer companies. But what is silicon? Essentially, it's just glass, made out of sand—one of the most abundant substances on the face of the earth. Again, it's human ingenuity that has turned sand into one of the most powerful engines of our modern, high-tech economy.

The same is true of penicillin. Sure, it cures sickness for people all over the world. But think about where it comes from: a mold. It took human ingenuity to make it valuable.

That's the magic of a free society—everyone can move forward and prosper because wealth comes from within. You don't need natural resources to start your own business; you need a good idea and the willingness to work very hard and make a lot of mistakes. We can all do that. And we need not focus on just the superstars of business, like the ones I have mentioned above. At home, in their communities, and in their places of work and worship, ordinary Americans come up with extraordinary new innovations every day—like the guy who invented Post-It Notes.

KISSING FROGS TO FIND A PRINCE

Art Fry liked to sing in his church choir. But he had a problem: the bookmarks in his hymnal kept falling out and he kept missing his cues. But Fry was a resourceful man. A 1984 *People* magazine profile captured his situation perfectly: "One Sunday, while daydreaming during a sermon, Fry, 53, a chemical engineer specializing in new product development for the 3M Company in St. Paul, Minnesota, had a flash of inspiration. He remembered a product a colleague discovered during an unsuccessful experiment—instead of a super strength adhesive, he'd come up with a low-tack glue. Racing back to the lab, Fry found the substance not quite perfect for his purposes—it peeled off easily but still left a residue on the page—but his quest was launched." Eventually Fry felt that he had perfected a product that would come to be known as those little yellow memo pads called Post-It Notes. The 3M marketing department was a little skeptical at first. Why, after all, would anyone need little pieces of paper with glue that *doesn't* stick? Fry convinced them—and the rest is history. Though its inventor has since retired, Post-It Notes are now a $1 billion business. As Fry himself put it, "You have to kiss a lot of frogs to find a prince."

> **That's the magic of a free society—everyone can move forward and prosper because wealth comes from within.**

In this new era more than ever before, it is what we create in our minds, in our imagination—stirred by our faith in the future—that is the real source of wealth. That's the exciting truth of the extraordinary changes that are coming. They remind us that it's people, not possessions, that warrant the highest value.

The key is to create an environment where freedom can flourish, where people can unleash the spirit of innovation within them, develop their true potential, learn the lessons of their own mistakes, and reap the rewards of their own success. That is why as we go into the twenty-first century, we need public policies that protect America's human capital and inspire young entrepreneurs. We also need leaders who are fundamentally committed to shifting money, power, and control from "they the government" back to "we the people."

CHAPTER FOUR

EDUCATION IN
THE INFORMATION AGE

EDUCATION IN THE Information Age is a whole different ball game from what it was in the Industrial Age. Why? Because the rules of society and business are changing—and sluggish, bureaucratic, one-size-fits-all school systems are not keeping up.

To help prepare our children to compete and succeed in the Information Age economy of the twenty-first century, we must start with the fundamental premise that the human mind is the real wellspring of capital, and there is a gold mine of wealth within each child.

Thus, our top priority must be creating a learning environment that helps every child develop his or her God-given potential. We need to create an environment of freedom, a world where every parent is free to choose schools that work—schools that are safe, clean, disciplined, drug-free, highly personalized, and academically challenging, and that reinforce rather than undermine the moral and spiritual values parents are trying to teach at home. We must also give teachers the freedom to create such an environment, without bureaucratic interference.

Today, knowledge is power. If a child masters the basics—reading, writing, arithmetic, and critical thinking—and truly learns how to learn, he or she will experience more opportunities and a higher standard of living than we as parents can possibly imagine. Well educated children will be able to take advantage of the emerging technology revolution. They will be able to adapt to a rapidly changing global marketplace. They will have the smarts and the discipline to start their own small businesses at home, at college, on family farms as well as in major population centers. They will have the confidence to embrace change, not shrink from it. For them, the digital age will hold enormous promise.

EQUIPPING CHILDREN TO SUCCEED
IN THE TWENTY-FIRST CENTURY

The danger is that children who are not equipped with a solid grasp of fundamental skills may very well be left behind in this new Information Age economy. Children who slip between the cracks of society in schools that don't work—with roofs that leak; books that are missing pages; and classrooms that are devoid of discipline and moral instruction, run by bureaucrats obsessed with "values clarification," "invented spelling," and "new math"—will suffer greatly. They will be cheated out of the opportunity to pursue the American dream. They will find themselves unable to comprehend—much less compete in—a society in which the mastery of information, not muscle, is the new source of wealth and power.

Sadly, such a divide between the knowledge "haves" and the knowledge "have nots" is already happening because too many of America's urban schools are a disaster. At many urban schools, there is little hope for children to be adequately educated. That's why so many urban parents want the freedom to put their children in better public schools, private schools, or even to teach their children at home.

Suburban and rural areas are not exempt from the troubles of American education. Today, in too many of these schools, test scores and basic skills are too low. High standards in reading, writing, and arithmetic have been systematically watered down. At the same time, too many schools are teaching a set of values that contradict what parents are trying to instill at home, while rapidly growing educational bureaucracies are diverting valuable resources away from classrooms.

This is morally unacceptable in a free society. Equipping our children with the skills and tools they need to compete and succeed in the twenty-first century must be a top priority. The status quo (what Ronald Reagan called "Latin for the mess we are in") won't do.

A BEACON OF HOPE

Education is a big deal in our house, as you can imagine it would be in any family with five daughters. It's also a big deal at *Forbes* magazine, because the truth is that we simply cannot remain the world's economic leader in the next century if our kids can't read and write well, much less excel at math and science. While I was finishing this book, I spoke at a conference of the American Management Association about human capital and the economy of the twenty-first century. While I was there, I learned some disturbing new facts. According to a survey the group had taken, 36 percent of job applicants tested by major American companies in 1998 lacked sufficient reading and math skills to do the job they sought, up from 23 percent in 1997 and 19 percent in 1996. Wholesale and retail companies had the toughest time finding qualified applicants, followed by manufacturers. This is a very serious problem, and it is getting worse rather than better.

Equipping our children with the skills and tools they need to compete and succeed in the twenty-first century must be a top priority.

This is the reason *Forbes* is continually running cover stories and major articles about trends in American education. It's also why for two decades I've been traveling all over the country to visit schools of all kinds—public, private, and parochial—looking for solutions rather than excuses.

In the fall of 1997, I found a gem on Harlem's West 121 Street. The Family Academy is an innovative little neighborhood school that's truly become a beacon of hope.

"I noticed way too many kids were entering eighth grade drastically deficient in reading and math skills," recalls Christina Giammalva, cofounder with David Liben and his wife, Meredith. "If the city was going to make progress in reducing its dropout rate of 60 percent to 70 percent, it seemed we should be starting with kids in kindergarten." So they did.

The Family Academy is a public school. But through a unique, charter school–like arrangement in Harlem, it is allowed to be run by the teachers like a private school. The teachers raise private funds to cover additional costs. They create their own curriculum (with a heavy emphasis on phonics). They design their own calendar (after-school programs run until 5 PM for eleven months a year). They choose their own dress code (uniforms, with dress-down Fridays). They also offer programs to help parents get ahead, such as marriage and family counseling, job placement, and high school equivalency training.

As the teachers told me themselves, the key to their success is creating a sense of real accountability to the parents and a warm, supportive community for the kids. No one forces kids to go to The Family Academy. Parents choose to send their kids there because they know the school will really educate and care for their children. Applicants are accepted through a random lottery with no pre-screening and no academic admissions requirement. Opened in 1991 with a handful of kindergartners, nearly four hundred students up through middle school now attend. All come from roughly a twelve-block radius around the school, and most are from single-parent families. Yet by 1996, Family Academy students had quadrupled their reading scores. Since then, reading scores have gone up even further and are now three times the neighborhood average.

But all that said, you would still have to see it to believe it— precious faces, excited about learning, being cared for, beginning to think that maybe, just maybe, they really do have a hope and a future... that maybe, just maybe, they do have a special gift, given to them by God, waiting to find expression, ready to take them out of poverty and on to exciting new adventures. These are not shy children. They are lively. They looked me straight in the eye when asking me questions and answering my questions. Real learning is going on in that school, and in my experience, that is a real sign of hope. Freedom works—imagine that!

SAVING OUR SCHOOLS

The big question now is this: Is it possible for parents and teachers to wrestle their schools away from the politicians and the bureaucracies so that America's children can truly compete and succeed in this Information Age economy? It's certainly not easy. In 1996, for example, New York City's Catholic leader, John Cardinal O'Connor, made a dramatic proposal to the public school system: Give us New York City's worst students, academically or disciplinarily, and let us show the world what Catholic schools can do. But the Big Apple's education establishment—in a stunning display of arrogance and contempt—sputtered excuses as to why it could not accept the cardinal's offer. In 1998 President Clinton vetoed a bill that would have allowed the low-income parents of two thousand children in Washington, D.C., to use federally funded scholarships worth up to $3,200 each to send their children to better schools. A poll found 65 percent of D.C. parents supportive of the program, and it was endorsed by the *Washington Post*. "A modest voucher experiment might help energize the public schools," noted the *Post's* editors. "People who think of vouchers as a way of somehow evading responsibility for public education are blowing smoke. And such a program, we believe, will not do harm to the system or by implication suggest that it is a permanent loser." But special-interest opposition killed the program, and thousands of children continue to languish in some of the nation's most horrible urban schools.

Still, I believe we can save our schools and put parents and teachers back in charge. But to be blunt, it is going to take some tough, courageous leaders who understand the times and know what America must do, because the special-interest groups who oppose real parental and teacher control of education are too powerful to be faced all alone. Most education reforms should occur at the local and state levels but the president has an important role to play. Specifically, the president must be prepared to vigorously and consistently:

- Promote K-12 education reform measures that strengthen state and local academic standards, enhance accountability, enforce real discipline, and put power back in the hands of parents and teachers, where it belongs. Such options include: a back-to-basics approach to math, reading, and science curricula; rigorous testing programs; fast-track teacher certification for qualified business and military professionals; higher pay for good teachers; public school choice options; charter schools; educational savings accounts; vouchers; private opportunity scholarships; tuition tax credits; and home schooling. Also, block granting federal education funds to states so parents, teachers, and community leaders can use the money to improve their local schools.

- Protect the legal rights of all parents and children from civil rights discrimination and educational discrimination.

- Support English immersion programs to help students learn to read, write, and speak in English as quickly as possible.

- Visit schools that work—and schools that are failing—and bring the national media along to highlight the good news and bad news in American education.

- Publicly honor parents and teachers who demonstrate heroism on the front lines of education.

- Encourage colleges and universities to create innovative elementary and secondary schools in America's inner cities. Also encourage pastors, priests, and rabbis to open more faith-based schools in urban neighborhoods. This will help expand the supply of quality educational opportunities right where they are needed most.

- Veto any idea that takes money and control away from parents and teachers and puts it into the hands of the special-interest groups who care more about power than people.

It is essential that a new generation of leaders come to the education reform discussion with the understanding that monopolies don't work in business, and they don't work in education. Morally, it is the right of parents—not bureaucrats or politicians—to decide what is best for their children. Financially, it is the right of taxpayers—not the government—to decide where and how their education dollars should be spent. These are the principles that must guide a real transformation of American education.

EMPOWERING PARENTS, EMPOWERING TEACHERS

Today's bureaucratically suffocated schools seldom see parents as "customers." Although parents pay taxes and their taxes pay for public schools, bureaucracies see government as their customer. Local, state, and federal government, after all, pay the bills, so the "educrats" pay an inordinate amount of time attending to political concerns, not parental ones.

The key to improving education is increasing accountability, and that means putting control of education dollars into the hands of parents and letting them choose the best school for their children. Some say parents can't be trusted to choose wisely for their children. But I could not disagree more. We are free to choose our spouses, our homes, and our professions. Why, then, can't parents be free to choose schools that work best for their own kids?

Some parents will keep their kids in the schools they attend now. Great. Other parents will choose public, private, or parochial schools that they feel are safer. Or that will improve math scores. Or that will provide better vocational training. Or give more attention to reading and writing skills. Or have great music programs. Or fantastic sports programs. Or provide strict discipline and instill respect for authority. That's great too. With parents choosing schools, schools will have to respond to the needs of parents—their customers—not bureaucrats and politicians.

PUBLIC SCHOOL CHOICE

Public school choice and charter schools are essential to improving public education. That's because most parents want to keep their children in the public school system—but they also eagerly want public schools to improve dramatically and respond to their needs and the needs of their children. Since 1990 more than 1,100 charter schools have been launched in thirty-four states and the District of Columbia. Two-thirds of these schools have waiting lists of students eager to get in. I can see why. I've visited numerous charter schools over the years, and most work remarkably well. In Phoenix, Arizona, for example, Lisa Graham Keegan—the state's superintendent of public instruction—took me to the Advantage Charter School. It's a model of high standards, strong values, firm discipline, and real results. Kids there are learning, and they seem to be having fun along the way.

The secret, according to Jeanne Allen of the Center for Education Reform, is giving teachers the freedom to create schools that meet the needs of parents and students. As stated on her website *www.edreform.com*: "Charter schools are independent public schools, designed and operated by educators, parents, community leaders, educational entrepreneurs, and others. They are sponsored by designated local or state educational organizations who monitor their quality and integrity, but allow them to operate free from the traditional bureaucratic and regulatory red tape that hogties public schools. Freed from such micromanagement, charter schools design and deliver programs tailored to educational excellence and community needs. Because they are schools of choice, they are held to the highest level of accountability—consumer demand."

PRIVATE SCHOOL CHOICE

Private school choice is also important, especially for those parents who live in the inner city, where private and parochial education is high quality and low cost. The good news is that at the state and local level, parents are beginning to win some very important victories. In Milwaukee, Wisconsin, for example, Governor Tommy Thompson and an African-American state legislator named Annette "Polly" Williams teamed up in the early 1990s to fight for educational freedom for low-income parents. After bruising political and legal battles, they helped create the nation's first private school choice program. Up to five thousand low-income children can now use publicly funded scholarships to attend private or religious schools of their parents' choice.

Clint Bolick is a lawyer who has represented the families fighting against the educational bureaucracy for the right to send their kids to good, safe schools. Throughout the myriad judicial proceedings, Bolick would always bring busloads of students and parents into the courtroom so everyone would understand that the lives of real people were being affected. In a 1992 speech, Bolick described the day he argued the case before the Wisconsin Supreme Court (which would later render a four-to-three decision approving the limited voucher program):

> When we had the argument in the Wisconsin Supreme Court, once again we arranged to get a busload of kids and parents to go to the argument in Madison. It turned out this time the bus was late, and by the time the kids

got there the courtroom was packed to capacity and there
was no place for them to sit. Most of the seats were occupied with bureaucrats who had taken the day off to come
and see the argument. Most of the people in the audience
were white and most of them had a vested interest in the
status quo.

Around two minutes to ten, when the argument
started, I looked to the back to see whether the kids had
arrived. The doors have glass panes, and I looked at the
doors and, sure enough, I saw this row of faces with their
noses pushed against the windows—these beautiful,
innocent, little faces. I thought to myself, what a
metaphor for what is going on in our society. All of these
little faces on the outside, always looking in.

The Milwaukee school choice program has become very popular with parents and students—72 percent of low-income parents in
Milwaukee support it. It has spawned a similar program in Cleve-
land, Ohio. It is also forcing the Milwaukee public schools to make
long overdue improvements. John Gardner, a member of the
Milwaukee Public School system's board of directors and a member of the National Association for the Advancement of Colored
People, submitted an affidavit in a subsequent court proceeding in
1996 in which he said:

> My involvement with Milwaukee Public Schools—as a
> member of the school board, as a parent, and as an active
> and concerned citizen—has persuaded me that MPS's
> internal reforms require the sustained challenge and
> competition of the Milwaukee Parental Choice Program.
> The program also puts effective pressure on MPS to
> expand, accelerate and improve reforms long deliberated
> and too-long postponed. The following examples
> demonstrate MPS's responsiveness to the needs and

requests of our low-income minority families during 1995–96:

- MPS has, at long last, approved its first charter school.
- We approved our third Montessori school, after more than a decade of long waiting lists [of students that want] to enter our two highly successful MPS Montessori schools.
- In an historic action, the MPS board voted to close six schools we identified as failing and to reconstitute these schools' administrations and faculties.
- We have contracted with two religiously affiliated, non-sectarian schools for exceptional education students.

Then, in December of 1998, came another sign that private school choice is helping to motivate the public schools to raise their standards and treat parents and students with dignity and respect. MPS Superintendent Alan Brown offered parents an extraordinary guarantee: the district will actually hire tutors for any student who stays in public schools but does not learn to read at grade level by the end of the second grade. The bottom line: parent-centered education reforms are not zero sum where private schools win and public schools lose; they help improve the quality of all schools and thus improve the quality of life for all children.

At the same time, all across the country, business and community leaders are teaming up to provide private opportunity scholarships for poor and disadvantaged students in urban areas. Pat Rooney, for example, a successful Indiana businessman in the health insurance business, is a pioneer of such privately funded educational scholarships. His Golden Rule Insurance company (the nation's leading Medical Savings Account company) has invested nearly $6 million in K-8 vouchers. Over seventeen hundred low-income Indianapolis children participate in the program, and more than four thousand are on a waiting list.

In New York City business leaders such as Peter Flanigan, Roger Hertog, Richard Gilder, Bruce Kovner, and Thomas Tisch run the School Choice Scholarships Foundation to help low-income children attend Catholic schools.

In Texas businessman James Leininger and public policy innovator Fritz Steiger teamed up in 1992 to launch CEO America to do something similar. In 1998 they committed $50 million over the next decade to help every child in San Antonio attend a school of his or her parents' choice, be it public, private, or parochial.

In Wisconsin public policy innovator Michael Joyce, the Lynde and Harry Bradley Foundation, and numerous business and community leaders have invested $20 million since 1992 to help low-income children attend private schools in a Milwaukee program entirely separate from the publicly funded program described above.

One of the most amazing examples I've seen of how eager urban parents are to get their kids in better schools occurred while I was writing this book. Ted Forstmann, who runs the Gulfstream Aerospace Company, and John Walton, an investor and son of Sam (Wal-Mart) Walton, announced in 1998 that their Children's Scholarship Fund (CSF) would contribute $100 million to create opportunity scholarships for forty thousand low-income children to go to schools of their parents' choice. What happened? More than 1.2 million people applied. By April of 1999 CSF had to use a lottery system to choose which K-8 children would receive the scholarships of between $600 and $1,600 per year for four years. Families are obliged to kick in any difference between the scholarship and the cost of tuition. Fortunately, many urban private schools cost less than $2,000 a year per student, with discounts for families enrolling several children.

The privately funded scholarship movement is "one of this decade's most dramatic examples of effective political and cultural leadership," wrote Adam Meyerson in his profile of such efforts in *Policy Review* magazine in January of 1999. He's absolutely right.

But with so many children still trapped in failing urban public schools, clearly much more must be done.

THE MINNESOTA MODEL

Another sign of educational freedom and hope comes from Minnesota. In 1997 Minnesota's then-governor, Arne Carlson, introduced a bold, dramatic, and bipartisan public education reform plan, "Students First," that passed the Minnesota House of Representatives by a vote of 108-21 and passed the state Senate by a vote of 50-9. The Minnesota plan made several key reforms. It increased the existing education tax deduction from $650 to $1,625 per child in kindergarten through sixth grade, and from $1,000 to $2,500 per child in grades seven through twelve. Private school tuition, fees, transportation, textbooks, and instructional materials are covered, as is academic summer school, tutoring, and educational computer materials. It also created a new refundable educational tax credit of $1,000 per child (up to $2,000 per family) for families with annual incomes under $33,500. Private school textbooks, instructional supplies, and tutoring were covered, but not tuition. The legislation expanded charter schools and public school choice programs and put new statewide testing and teacher accountability measures into place.

How did parents win such dramatic new control over their public schools? They elected a chief executive who made their interests his top priority. In December of 1996 Governor Carlson set forth his proposal and slowly began to build public support for it. I endorsed "Students First" in February of 1997 and publicized the governor's efforts through media interviews, radio advertising, and on the web. Minnesota-based organizations mobilized to get the word out and soon launched a massive public relations campaign to explain the plan and persuade fellow Minnesotans to support it. Mitchell Pearlstein and Kristin Robbins of Minnesotans for School Choice; Dr. Ed Johnson, Jr., of the Minnesota Association of Christian Schools; Tom Prichard of the Minnesota Family Council; Pam von Gohren of the Minnesota Association of Christian Home Educators; Mike Ricci of CEF, Inc.; David Roth, representing the Lutheran Schools; and Father David McCauley of the Minnesota Catholic Conference all put together an effective and persuasive grassroots coalition.

Meanwhile, Governor Carlson cajoled state legislators around the clock. When the state legislature passed an education budget bill that did not achieve his objectives, he vetoed it and sent it back to the drawing board. When the legislature saw how serious the governor really was, and when they saw how effective the public persuasion and mobilization efforts were, they finally passed the governor's plan.

The result was a shot heard 'round the educational world—one of the biggest victories for parents' rights to date—and the plan and politics of making it a reality are a model from which other states can learn. In fact, Governor Jeb Bush has already moved quickly to enact even bolder parental-freedom reforms in Florida.

ENGLISH FOR THE CHILDREN

In 1998 another important educational freedom initiative—known as Proposition 227, or "English for the Children"—was passed by the voters of California. Few national leaders weighed in on this issue. But I endorsed it because it went to the heart of restoring the proper relationship between parents and children and the state.

For years there has been enormous frustration among parents and teachers with the bilingual educational system in California, and for good reason. The state spends about a half-billion dollars a year on bilingual education, yet only 5 percent of the children in these programs become proficient in English every year, suggesting a 95 percent failure rate. One out of every four children in California's public schools can't speak English—double the number of ten years ago—and the reason isn't because these children can't learn. It's because the system isn't doing its job.

The English for the Children initiative proposed requiring all children in California public schools to be taught in English. It proposed giving parents the freedom to choose to keep their children in bilingual programs, if they so desired. It also proposed providing funding for English tutoring assistance for those children most in need.

English is the language of economic opportunity, here and around the globe. If you know English, the Information Age is your friend. If you know English, the doors of opportunity are wide open. But if you don't, you're stuck—and in danger of being left behind.

That's why conservatives *and* liberals, Democrats *and* Republicans, joined together to make sure that all children in California—regardless of their background—would have the opportunity to learn English, get a solid education, and move ahead.

The grassroots coalition driving the campaign was as fascinating as it was diverse: Ron Unz, a conservative businessman and high-tech entrepreneur; Jaime Escalante, whose remarkable story of teaching calculus to Hispanic children at Garfield High School in East Los Angeles was turned into the inspiring film *Stand and Deliver*; Fernando Vega, a longtime leader in the California Latino community who was chosen by the Clinton-Gore campaign in 1992 to turn out the Latino vote in the San Francisco area; Alice Callaghan, an activist, a minister, and a devout liberal; and Gloria Matta Tuchman, a mother and elementary school teacher with over thirty years' experience teaching children to read, write, and speak English.

Sadly, the president and vice president opposed the English for the Children initiative. In so doing, they turned a deaf ear to all the parents who are fed up with a system that is ruining the hopes and dreams of young people throughout California. To me, it was a tell-tale sign of career politicians who have been in Washington too long. The educational bureaucracy in California also fought to destroy the initiative, using millions of dollars in teachers' union dues. Thousands of rank-and-file California teachers personally supported the initiative. But still their own dues were used by their unions to fight against their own personal views. I believe that was wrong: No one should be forced to fund a political campaign with which he or she disagrees.

Still, when all was said and done, the English for the Children initiative passed overwhelmingly, with 61 percent of the vote. Now even critics are beginning to admit that the new English-immersion programs are helping students learn English faster and better than they had expected. "I honestly didn't expect to see [the kids] achieve as well as they are doing," said Jose Posada, a teacher at the Los Angeles Elementary School in Koreatown, in a January 1999 interview with the *Los Angeles Times*. "Many of us who believed in the bilingual education program were scared about the unknowns. Now we're saying, 'Well, maybe it's not so bad. Maybe it's time we start talking about the positives.'" Yomy Duran, a teacher at the Dena Elementary School in southeast Los Angeles, told a reporter, "I expected that [the children's] self-esteem would be affected, and that they would feel inhibited, give up easily. Instead, they are excited, motivated." Another *Los Angeles Times* article in February of 1999 reported that "children are absorbing English at such a rapid rate that in many places it is the language of choice on the playground, at the lunch table and in line for the bus." It is just the beginning, of course, but these are clearly steps in the right direction.

HOME SCHOOLING—
TEACHING CHILDREN WITH EXCELLENCE

Still another sign of hope is the success of America's home schooling movement. More than one million American kids are being taught at home by their own parents, and a study released in early 1999 proved what most observers already knew: Home schooling works. The survey found that home schooled children scored well above the national median on standardized tests. It also found that kids of parents who had not been certified to teach did as well as those whose parents had such credentials.

The phenomenon of home schooling is a wonderful example of the American can-do attitude. Growing numbers of parents have become disenchanted with government-run public schools. Most who can afford to do so put their kids in private or parochial schools. But many parents have simply taken matters into their own hands, literally, and their children are getting first-class educations. Critics carp that these children may suffer from a lack of "socialization," which in plain English means that they are not around their friends all day. But in most cases, these kids do interact with peers through Scouting, Little League, dance lessons, and the like. The real danger to these kids isn't a lack of "socialization"; it's the threat of new government restrictions aimed at hobbling the home schooling movement. We must guard against such Washington-knowsbest interference and protect the freedom of parents to teach their children with excellence.

Our job now is to remove the political obstacles that stand in the way, and set parents, teachers, and children free.

EDUCATION: THE PASSPORT TO ECONOMIC FREEDOM

The truth is, I'm an optimist. I believe that parents and teachers all over the country understand—even if the establishment politicians don't—that as we head into an exciting new century and a rapidly changing global economy, a good education is a civil right and a passport to economic freedom. People understand that we need to prepare our children to compete and succeed, and that some of the old systems are failing the very kids who need the most help.

"I can't presume to know exactly what my uncle would say about the current debate over school vouchers and choice," wrote Alveda King, the niece of Dr. Martin Luther King, Jr., and a leader in the fight for parental control of education, in a September 1997 essay in the *Wall Street Journal*. "But I know what principles he taught, and I know that he not only preached but also practiced them. Martin Luther King, Jr. and his siblings were products of public and private schools—and impressed upon my generation the importance of faith and family in effective schooling."

"Indeed, all Americans should want the public schools to be the very best they can be," Ms. King concluded. "But we must make it possible for all people to choose the best educational settings for their children, no matter what their circumstances." She is absolutely right.

Our job now is to remove the political obstacles that stand in the way, and set parents, teachers, and children free. It won't be easy, but it's the right thing to do.

CHAPTER FIVE

TEAR DOWN
THIS TAX CODE

I COME FROM a family of entrepreneurs and risk-takers—of tax-*payers*, not tax-*raisers*. And so do you.

That's why I believe so strongly that it is time to send the monstrous, anti-family, anti-freedom federal income tax code to the ash heap of history. We need a new tax code for a new century, one that rewards—not punishes—hard work, creativity, innovation, savings, and investment. The current system is corruptingly complex. It threatens to keep us from making the most of this new economic era. And it has hurt far too many people for far too long.

IRS—THE POWER TO DESTROY

In August of 1996, after nine years of being harassed and intimidated by the Internal Revenue Service (IRS) over disputed back taxes, Shirley Barron's husband, Bruce, took his own life. The IRS "sits, does nothing, and watches you die," Mr. Barron wrote in his suicide note.

As the Associated Press reported: "The Barrons' tax troubles began when they lost an $80,000 investment in a recycling company in the 1980s. Their accountant said they could deduct it on their taxes, but the IRS told them two years later that they had to pay, and interest and penalties began mounting. Mrs. Barron said the agency began forcing the clients of her husband's law firm to pay the agency directly, humiliating him and harming his business. She also said that her husband tried to negotiate a settlement, but that the agency continued to pursue him."

Incredibly, even suicide did not stop the IRS. When I met Mrs. Barron at a tax reform town hall meeting in Bedford, New Hampshire, in February of 1998, she told me the IRS had just sent her late husband a new letter demanding payment within ten days for about $1,000 in back taxes. Incensed, she called the IRS to tell them they had just sent a tax bill to a dead person. They hung up on her. Then they placed a lien on her bank accounts.

"We didn't realize that we had just embarked on the road to hell," she said, explaining how she and her husband had tried to pay off their tax bills without going into bankruptcy. "They inflicted Gestapo-type tactics on Bruce and me even when we worked within their system."

The IRS had just sent her late husband a new letter demanding payment within ten days for about $1,000 in back taxes. She called the IRS to tell them they had just sent a tax bill to a dead person. They hung up on her. Then they placed a lien on her bank accounts.

Eventually, the IRS agreed to an out-of-court settlement of Mrs. Barron's $1 million wrongful death suit against them.

Monsignor Lawrence Ballweg has also experienced the wrath of the IRS. Retired now, the monsignor was a Catholic priest in New York City for over five decades. When his mother passed away in 1988, her will established a charitable trust to help the poor and named him as the trustee. The monsignor spent hundreds of hours every year completing the necessary paperwork. But in the spring of 1996, the IRS informed him that he was not filling out the tax forms correctly. They sent him more forms to complete. In November of 1996, the IRS then sent the monsignor a notice that he now owed more than $18,000 in taxes and penalties. Three months later, in January of 1997, the IRS informed him that it intended to seize his bank account, automobile, and other property. Finally, after CNN publicized his story, the IRS informed him that he did not owe any tax after all.

The monsignor testified of his tax code travails at the Senate hearing on IRS abuses in the fall of 1997. Joining him were other Americans from all over the country who spoke of the terrible treatment they had received at the hands of their own government. Perhaps even more chilling was the testimony of current and former IRS agents, some wearing black masks, others hiding behind dark screens and disguising their voices electronically, each describing unbelievable but true tales of government corruption and deceit. The nation was stunned. How could this happen in America, the land of the free?

The U.S. federal income tax code, with its attendant regulations, is over 7,000,000 words and rising. No one knows what is in there.

Sadly, these IRS horror stories are not isolated events. Rather they are symptomatic of an unfathomable federal income tax code with 569 different forms and 17,000 pages of complicated rules and regulations. Just to put it into perspective, Lincoln's Gettysburg Address, which defined the American nation, was a little over 200 words in length. The Declaration of Independence is about 1,300 words long. The Holy Bible is about 773,000 words. But the U.S. federal income tax code, with its attendant regulations, is over 7,000,000 words and rising. No one knows what is in there. Give your tax information to fifty different accountants, and you will get fifty different returns. And it is precisely this murkiness that breeds police-state collection tactics. Who can effectively argue with the IRS if no one understands the system? Who can successfully fight with an IRS so large and so powerful?

"No federal agency touches the lives of more Americans than the Internal Revenue Service," writes Senate Finance Committee Chairman William Roth, Jr., of Delaware in his 1999 book, *The Power To Destroy*. "None strikes as much fear into the hearts of honest taxpayers. The threat of an audit, pronounced by the awesome power of the IRS, looms over the head of every individual who files a return. With an army of over 100,000 employees, and a budget exceeding $7 billion, the Internal Revenue Service has more manpower than all other federal law enforcement agencies combined."

It is not right. Yet this is the tax system that the establishment chooses to defend. In doing so, it is defending an entire culture of political pollution, corruption, and dishonesty. It is a culture that preys upon the weak—auditing poor families, many of whom live in the South, who earn less than $25,000 a year. It is a culture that takes advantage of single parents (mostly women) and small business owners and hounds them mercilessly—sometimes seizing their bank accounts, closing down their shops, and driving them into bankruptcy. It is a culture that draws over sixty-seven thousand lobbyists to Washington, D.C., like mosquitoes to a swamp.

It is also a culture that takes more money from the American people than at any other point in our nation's history. The federal tax burden has risen a staggering 45 percent per person since 1992, according to the nonpartisan Tax Foundation—rising to $6,690 from $4,625. Add in state and local taxes, and the total U.S. tax burden in 1998 was $9,881 per person. Even during the peak years of World War II and the Korean War, Washington did not tax American workers as heavily as it does today. Federal tax receipts in 1998 hit an all-time record of 21.7 percent of gross domestic product. When the current administration first took office, federal taxes consumed only 19 percent of our national economy.

This crushing burden is fueled in part by the 1990 and 1993 tax increases—the latter was the largest tax increase in American history—and in part by the "progressivity" of the tax code, which ensures that no matter how fast a worker's income is growing, his federal income taxes will grow even faster. On top of all this is the massive cost of complying with the tax code. Americans spend some 5.4 billion hours each year filling out IRS paperwork. Compliance costs are now an estimated $250 billion annually, according to the Tax Foundation. A March 1999 Associated Press poll found that 56 percent of Americans now pay someone else to complete their tax returns. The rich can more easily absorb these costs and inconveniences; it is low- and middle-income workers who get hit the hardest.

ABOLISH THE IRS

Such an abomination as this tax code should never be tolerated in a free society. It would be morally and fiscally unsustainable at any time in history. But it is particularly destructive as we move into this new Information Age economy. If we are going to make it simpler and easier for people to live their own lives and run their own businesses—if we are going to reward rather than punish America's new era of entrepreneurs—and if we are going to remain economically secure and prosperous in a new and very challenging global economic environment, then we need to make some fundamental changes right away.

We can't tinker with this tax code monstrosity or try to reform it around the edges. The only thing we can do with this hideous beast is kill it, drive a stake through its heart, bury it, and hope that it never rises again to terrorize the American people!

When I announced on September 22, 1995, that I was running for the Republican presidential nomination, few people took my candidacy seriously. After all, I was a mere asterisk in the polls, and I was vowing to junk the federal income tax code and replace it with a simple, honest, fair flat tax that's a real tax cut. The Washington political establishment and the "wise men" in the media just snickered, figuring I was on a fool's errand. But they forgot to factor in one thing: the disgust of the American people with the current system and politics as usual.

"We can't tinker with this tax code monstrosity or try to reform it around the edges," I told audiences in Iowa, New Hampshire, and elsewhere. "The only thing we can do with this hideous beast is kill it, drive a stake through its heart, bury it, and hope that it never rises again to terrorize the American people!" It was electric. Time after time, audiences leapt to their feet with standing ovations. Finally, someone had the courage to tell the truth. Finally, someone was speaking for working families who felt like they had no voice in Washington—no lobbyist, no lawyer, no lifetime politician who truly looked out for their interests. Taking my message directly to the American people in person, on television, on radio, and through the news media, I hammered away at the biggest source of political pollution and corruption and the biggest deadweight on families and businesses in America today and offered an honest, simple alternative in the form of the flat tax.

People are sick and tired of business-as-usual, and they don't want a "friendlier" IRS; they want *no* IRS.

The Republican establishment considered the idea a dangerous rebellion. Instead of embracing this pro-growth, pro-freedom agenda, the empire struck back and tried to destroy the message and the messenger. Both survived the onslaught. *Time* and *Newsweek* ran cover stories on the grassroots excitement over my flat tax message. The voters of Delaware and Arizona gave our campaign stunning, come-from-behind primary victories over the established front-runners. Exit polls showed that most Republican voters favored fundamental tax simplification and pro-growth, pro-family tax cuts. Senator Dole eventually embraced a 15 percent across-the-board tax cut as a down payment to more dramatic tax simplification, and "end the IRS as we know it" became a rallying cry for the GOP—and even for Ross Perot. We did not win the nomination that year, but we had reshaped the national debate with our positive, substantive, forward-looking message of hope, growth, and opportunity.

Since then, the Washington political establishment seems to have forgotten whatever it may have learned that year. The excuse of politicians used to be that "we can't cut taxes or simplify the system because of the deficit." Now the excuse is that "we can't cut taxes or simplify the system because of the surplus." The truth is that without strong, principled, and committed executive leadership, real tax simplification and relief just is not going to happen because the special interest groups and the forces of the status quo are too strong to be taken on haphazardly. Just look at what has happened in recent years: Lukewarm leadership in Washington has allowed the tax code to become even more complicated while claiming to make the IRS more friendly.

All this has just deepened my resolve. For wherever I travel around the country, I don't find any public sentiment for more tax code tinkering. People are sick and tired of business-as-usual, and they don't want a "friendlier" IRS; they want *no* IRS.

After my campaign I was sitting on an airplane next to a machinist who worked for one of the major airlines. He was hitching a ride from one facility to another. It was the end of the day and I was finished with my "preaching," so I let him do the talking. He told me that he's married, has two children, and earns a very good wage. But it's not enough. He has to work part-time, as well. His wife has to work part-time, too, not out of choice but out of necessity. On paper, he said, they are doing very well. But they worry that they're not spending enough time with their children, and they can't seem to get ahead of the curve.

Then he said he finally figured it out. He said, "It's those [expletive deleted] taxes. If you add up what you pay in federal income tax; federal payroll tax; state income tax; sales taxes; property taxes; gasoline taxes; utility taxes; you stay at a hotel, you pay occupancy taxes; you want to get married, you pay a fee; you want to drive, you pay a fee; you want a pet, you pay a fee." He said: "It's not just what they take out of your paycheck. Everything you do, the government gets a slice." He figured that over half their income went to the government by way of taxes and fees. That's why they seemed unable to get ahead of the curve even though they were willing to work so many hours. Is this freedom?

A NEW TAX CODE
FOR A NEW CENTURY

The fact is that working families and small business owners deserve the freedom to keep more of what they earn and not live as subjects of their own government. And I am more convinced than ever that the flat tax is the way to go.

Why? Because the flat tax is honest—no more loopholes, tax shelters, and unfair favors for the politically well-connected and the special-interest groups. Shouldn't every American be treated equally, fairly, and with dignity and respect?

The flat tax is so simple that you could fill out your taxes on a postcard. People have enough demands on their time these days.

The Steve Forbes Flat Tax Form

Individual Wage Tax   1999

Last name	First name and initial	(If joint return, also give spouse's name)	Your Social Security Number

Present Home Address (Number and Street including apartment number or rural route)		Spouse's Social Security Number

City, Town or Post Office, State and Zip code	Your occupation
	Spouse's occupation

1. Wages & Salary	1	
2. Number of adults in family	2	
3. Number of children in family	3	
4. Deductions for adults (multiply line 2 by $13,000)	4	
5. Deductions for children (multiply line 3 by $5,000)	5	
6. Total deductions (line 4 plus line 5)	6	
7. Taxable income (line 1 minus line 6)	7	
8. Tax (multiply line 7 by 17%)	8	

Why should people be forced to spend days and weeks filling out all kinds of complicated forms, always fearing that if they make a mistake they will find themselves face to face with the IRS?

THE FLAT TAX IS PRO-FAMILY

The flat tax is also a real tax cut for hardworking American families. Some critics say it's an attack on the middle class, but nothing could be further from the truth. Under my plan, each adult would have a generous personal exemption of $13,000. Each child would have an exemption of $5,000. That means a family of four earning $36,000 would pay no federal income tax—a tax cut of more than $1,600. That's real money that could be used to pay off credit card debts, cover medical expenses, hire a reading tutor, buy a home computer, or sock away for retirement. In fact, my plan would take about twenty million low-income Americans off the federal income tax rolls altogether, where they never should have been in the first place. Any money earned above the generous personal exemptions would be taxed at a low, fair 17 percent. There would be no tax on personal savings; no tax on Social Security benefits; no tax on pensions; no tax on dividends; no tax on capital gains on sale of assets such as homes, farms, stocks and family businesses; no "death taxes"; no alternative minimum tax; and no marriage tax penalty. Why should we go into a new century punishing hard work, saving, investment, retirement, and marriage? It makes no sense morally or economically.

THE FLAT TAX IS PRO-GROWTH

In addition to being a great boon for working families, the flat tax will also be a great boon for American businesses. With a flat tax there will be no tax on basic operating expenses such as the purchases of goods, services, and materials. There will be no tax on wages, salaries, and pensions. And there will be no tax on the purchase of capital equipment, structures, and land. All this will be deducted from gross revenues. The remaining income will be taxed at a simple, low rate of 17 percent. There are no complicated investment depreciation schedules. Instead, there will be immediate expensing, and unused expensing can be carried forward. There will be no complicated and anti-growth alternative minimum tax and no capital gains tax. Experts believe interest rates will fall significantly. Plus, the new system is so simple, it will virtually eliminate the $250 billion we spend every year complying with the tax code. If we phase-in such a system—with a transition plan that is fair and cost-effective to American businesses that have made major decisions based on the current rules—then I believe we can truly position ourselves for a new century of tremendous growth and innovation.

Even critics of the flat tax agree that such reforms will boost the American economy. They disagree only on the size of the boost. But

HOW MUCH MONEY WOULD YOUR FAMILY *SAVE* EVERY YEAR BY USING THE FLAT TAX?

With generous personal exemptions for adults and children—and a single, low tax rate of 17 percent—a well-constructed flat tax is a real tax cut for working families.

Annual Income	What You Owe The IRS Under Current Tax Code	What You Would Save Under The Steve Forbes 17% Flat Tax	Tax Cut
$30,000	$770.00	$770.00	100.0%
$36,000	$1,670.00	$1,670.00	100.0%
$40,000	$2,270.00	$1,590.00	70.0%
$50,000	$3,770.00	$1,390.00	36.9%
$60,000	$5,270.00	$1,190.00	22.6%
$70,000	$7,907.50	$2,127.50	26.9%
$80,000	$10,707.50	$3,227.50	30.1%
$90,000	$13,507.50	$4,327.50	32.0%
$100,000	$16,307.50	$5,427.50	33.3%

WHAT WOULD BE YOUR EFFECTIVE TAX RATE UNDER THE FLAT TAX?

With generous personal exemptions included in a well-constructed flat tax plan, much of a working family's income would not be taxed at all. Only the income earned above the generous personal exemptions would be taxed. That means that rather than paying a 17 percent tax rate, most working families would pay an effective tax rate of well under 10 percent.

Annual Income	Effective Flat Tax Rate
$30,000	0.0%
$36,000	0.0%
$40,000	1.7%
$50,000	4.8%
$60,000	6.8%
$70,000	8.3%
$80,000	9.4%
$90,000	10.2%
$100,000	10.9%
$250,000	14.6%
$500,000	15.8%
$1,000,000	16.4%
$5,000,000 – plus	17.0%

Assumes a married couple with two children under seventeen years old claiming the standard deduction and the new child tax credits versus a 17 percent flat tax plan with generous exemptions of $13,000 for each adult and $5,000 for each child.

as Dan Mitchell of The Heritage Foundation says, "It is worth noting that an increase in the growth rate of just one-half of one-percentage point would boost an average family of four's yearly income by more than $5,000 after ten years."

FREQUENTLY ASKED QUESTIONS

As I travel about the country, meeting with mom-and-pop store owners, factory workers, seniors, and CEOs, I find people are really excited by the prospect of such an honest, simple new system. I also find that they have lots of questions.

What will happen to charitable giving, for example? With a flat tax, I believe that we will see a surge of new charitable giving. Americans don't need to be bribed by the tax code to do what is in their hearts. We are a very generous people, and history proves that when people have more money, they give more to charity. With a flat tax, people will be free to keep more of what they earn. In turn, they will be free to give more to those who need it most. Remember, charitable giving went up significantly during the 1980s when President Reagan cut taxes and the economy grew.

What will happen to home buying in America? With a flat tax, I believe that new home construction and the sales of existing homes will grow impressively and that we will see more first-time home buyers than ever before. Why? Because a strong, growing economy is always good for home sales and home values. With more money in people's pockets, lower interest rates, and no tax on personal savings, it will be far easier for young people to build up enough money to put a down payment on their first home and to make the subsequent monthly payments.

Why not scrap the income tax altogether and go with a national sales tax? The problem is simple: we cannot trust the Washington political establishment to repeal the 16th Amendment to the U.S. Constitution, which authorizes the income tax. That would be the worst of both worlds. Also, a national sales tax would impose a very heavy burden on low- and middle-income workers and would force states that do not currently have a sales tax (like New Hampshire) to create a whole new tax-collecting bureaucracy on behalf of the federal government. So, while a national sales tax does have some merit (and some very devoted followers), I believe that the flat tax is easier to adopt.

There are, of course, lots of horror stories out there about the flat tax. Such attacks are fueled by a Washington political establishment that despises change and innovation. In fact, if you listen to the critics you will probably become convinced that the flat tax will destroy all that is good and decent in the world, cause your hair to fall out, and cause your dog to have fleas. It is all ridiculous, of course. But no one ever said that the image of politicians trying to hold onto power was a pretty picture.

MORE FREEDOM, LESS FRUSTRATION

So here is what I propose. Let's give every American the freedom to choose between filing under the old system or under the new flat tax system. Most people would immediately see how the flat tax saves them time and money and keeps the IRS out of their lives.

People already see it. Every day I get a flood of faxes, e-mail, and snail mail from people frustrated by the current tax system. In the fall of 1997 I received a particularly poignant e-mail from a newly-wed husband in Pennsylvania:

> Dear Mr. Forbes:
>
> I just got married two weeks ago and have just returned from my honeymoon. I am a graduate student so I don't make too much money but I do pretty well. My wife makes slightly more than I do as a computer programmer but she still doesn't make enough to bump us into the next tax bracket when her income is combined with mine.
>
> We sat down last night and talked about taxes because we both filled out new W-4 forms reflecting our marital status change. We were absolutely stunned to learn that being married is a penalty in our situation. The problem comes in under the standard deduction that one takes if one does not itemize on their taxes. If you are single, the number last year was $4,000. When married filing jointly, the number was $6,700. Well, it is easy to do the math and see that being married is a penalty.

For example, if you take two couples with identical combined income with one single and living together and one married, both have presumably identical living expenses (they both have to eat and they already live under the same roof). However, come tax time, the married couple can only exempt $6,700 from their tax return while the single couple can deduct $4,000 each, or $8,000 from their income. This results in a total net gain for the single couple of $1,300 of extra income that they do not have to claim on their taxes. It may not seem like much, but for us, it makes it very difficult for us to stay in the current tax bracket.

This is all bad enough, but in addition I just found out that if we don't get our withholding correct they will penalize me for not paying enough on time. Excuse me, but I was under the impression that 1) what we earned was our money, not the federal government's; and 2) that taxes weren't due until April 15! Can you explain to me how this is legal?

I am sorry to bore you with this example, as I am sure you are very well aware of this inconsistency in the tax code already (obviously since your organization is based on the only *fair* way to collect taxes, a flat tax), but I just wanted to let you know that this has cemented in stone my scorn for the way our government collects taxes and it really illustrates just how bloated and powerful the federal government has become.

Finally, a little commentary on the implications of this whole thing. It's my opinion that any society that penalizes marriage between a woman and a man (either financially or socially) is headed for destruction….

Please keep up the good work and keep on fighting for a flat tax. It is only fair.

My great-grandparents Robert and Agnes Forbes with B. C. Forbes (far right) and his siblings.

My grandparents Adeliade and B. C. Forbes with my father and three of his four brothers.

My grandmother Adeliade and grandfather B. C. Forbes on a return trip to Europe.

My grandfather B. C. Forbes typing his column.

My mother and father, Roberta and Malcolm Forbes, on their wedding day.

My father Malcolm in his office at Forbes, Inc.

Sabina and I.

My daughters (from left) Roberta, Moira, Catherine, Elizabeth, and Sabina; and my wife Sabina at our home in New Jersey.

With my daughter Elizabeth on the campaign bus in 1996.

My mother Roberta with two of her granddaughters, Isabelle and Elizabeth.

My five daughters (from left): Roberta, Sabina, Moira, Catherine, and Elizabeth.

On the campaign trail in New Hampshire with daughter Catherine in 1996.

Participating in a class at The Family Academy in Harlem, New York City.

Greeting a group of students in New Hampshire in 1996.

At the 75th anniversary of Forbes with former President Ronald Reagan and former Soviet Premier Mikhail Gorbachev.

Greeting General Colin Powell.

Interviewing former Chancellor of Germany Helmut Kohl.

A meeting with former President of Poland Lech Walesa.

Arriving with former Prime Minister Margaret Thatcher in Des Moines, Iowa, in 1998.

Conversing with former President Ronald Reagan.

Greeting Pope John Paul II at the Vatican in Rome, Italy.

Attending the Reagan library dedication with former presidents Bush, Reagan, Carter, and Ford.

In the spring of 1999 I went to Baltimore to meet with a number of black pastors from various major churches from around the country. I shared with them some of my thoughts about the state of our culture, especially after the Littleton, Colorado, tragedy. But what was one of the first issues that I was asked about when I opened the session up for discussion? Taxes. "Mr. Forbes, the folks in my congregation are beginning to move forward and achieve some success," one pastor told me. "But the better they do, the more they are running up against things like the capital gains tax that is really hurting their ability to grow their businesses. And then they start thinking about how to pass on some of their newly-found wealth to their children, and they're running into these incredibly high inheritance taxes. How are black folks supposed to get ahead in this country if Washington keeps taking away what they're working so hard to create?" It was a great question, spoken from the heart of a man who understands far better than the political establishment that what all Americans want—and deserve—is the freedom to create real wealth for themselves and their families and the freedom to pass it on to future generations.

WASHINGTON'S DIRTY LITTLE SECRET

If you understand just one principle about taxes, you will be ahead of most economists and policy makers in Washington and in state capitols around America. Taxes are not only a means of collecting revenue for the government—taxes are also a price and a burden. A tax on income, savings, and capital gains is the price you pay for working; for being successful, innovative, and productive; and for being willing to take risks, create new jobs, and lay a foundation for the future. And the proposition goes like this: If you raise the price or burden on these good things, you get less of them. If you lower the price, you get more of them. It's just that simple.

This is not a partisan issue. Every time in American history that we've lowered the tax burden, the American people have responded with energy, imagination, and innovation. The standard of living has improved, better jobs were created, and government revenues have gone up, not down. The dramatic 25 percent across-the-board Reagan-era tax cuts, for example, brought America out of a decade of economic stagnation and "malaise," created eighteen million new jobs, and set into motion an era of prosperity that we are still enjoying today. As Thomas Sowell, the brilliant scholar at the Hoover Institution in California (and a *Forbes* columnist), points out in his book *The Vision of the Anointed*: "Contrary to the notion that deficits have resulted from reduced tax receipts by the federal government, those receipts in fact reached new record highs during the Reagan administration. Every year of that administration saw the federal government collect more money than in any year of any previous administration in history. By the last year of the Reagan administration in 1988, the federal government collected over $391 billion *more* than during any year of the Carter administration—in percentage terms, the government took in 76 percent more that year than it had ever collected in any year of any other administration." So why did we have large deficits? Washington "spending increases simply outstripped the rising volume of tax receipts," observed Sowell, proving that "there is no amount of money that cannot be overspent."

> **Every time in American history that we've lowered the tax burden, the American people have responded with energy, imagination, and innovation.**

This gets to the dirty little secret in Washington: What the politicians really fear from tax relief and tax simplification is not a loss of revenue. They know in their hearts that the economy would expand and revenues would go up. What they really fear is a loss of power.

GROWING MOMENTUM

So while an honest, simple flat tax is essential to a new birth of freedom, it is not enough by itself. We also must keep the budget spending caps in place to impose real fiscal discipline. And we must pass a strong tax limitation amendment that would require a two-thirds super-majority vote of Congress in order to raise taxes. In the event Congress declared war, or a joint resolution to engage in military conflict, the provision could be waived. But in peacetime, such an amendment would make it extraordinarily difficult for Congress to raise taxes. In fact, four of the last five major tax increases would have been defeated had this tax limitation provision been in place.

If real tax cuts and tax simplification are somehow inconvenient to Washington, our response should be: So what? It is high time that Washington gets its priorities right. Our federal government exists to serve the needs of the nation; the nation should not always have to feed the endless appetites of the Washington politicians.

This is why support has steadily grown over the years for the flat tax—because people are looking for a simpler, easier, less expensive way. I first began advocating the flat tax in the early 1980s. But I was not the first to do so, and I have not been alone. Milton Friedman wrote about the flat tax in his book *Capitalism and Freedom* way back in 1962. Professors Alvin Rabushka and Robert Hall pioneered a modern version in their book *The Flat Tax*. Congressmen and senators from both political parties have introduced their own variations over the years. Most notable have been the efforts of Representative Dick Armey of Texas and Senator Richard Shelby of Alabama, who first introduced their version in 1994.

The dirty little secret in Washington: What the politicians really fear from tax relief and tax simplification is not a loss of revenue. What they really fear is a loss of power.

In his 1995 memoir of his life covering eleven presidents, twenty-two political conventions, and decades of palace intrigue in our nation's capital, veteran ABC News journalist David Brinkley concluded that the flat tax is the only way to clean up all the corruption and complexity in the tax code. "What I have found is that only one idea for tax reform

comes anywhere close to genuinely wide acceptance by the taxpayers, and that is the flat tax," he wrote. "Why? Many reasons.... Its
greatest virtue is simplicity."

In 1996 the National Commission on Economic Growth and Tax
Reform chaired by Jack Kemp "recommended to the Congress and to
the President of the United States that the current Internal Revenue
Code be repealed in its entirety. The present system is beyond
repair—it is impossibly complex, outrageously expensive, overly intru-
sive, economically destructive, and manifestly unfair." In its place,
the commission urged the adoption of "a single, low rate tax with a
generous personal exemption" that would "lower the tax burden on
America's working families and remove it on those least able to pay."

TEAR DOWN THIS TAX CODE

In the fall of 1997—not long after my campaign and just after the
first in a series of Senate hearings on IRS corruption—a new piece
of legislation called the "Tax Code Termination Act" was introduced in Congress. Its sponsors were Representatives Steve Largent
of Oklahoma and Bill Paxon of New York, and Senators Tim
Hutchinson of Arkansas and Sam Brownback of Kansas (who won
former Senator Dole's seat). I endorsed it immediately and launched
an eight-week, fourteen-state "Tax Code Termination Tour" and a
series of radio advertising campaigns to promote it. Why? Because
it would require Congress to pass a new tax code and abolish the old
one by 2002. The new system would be required to meet seven critical goals:

1. Apply a single low rate to all taxpayers
2. Require a super-majority of both the House and Senate before
   raising taxes
3. Provide tax relief for working Americans
4. Protect the rights of taxpayers and end collection abuses
5. Eliminate the bias against savings and investment

6. Promote economic growth and job creation

7. Protect the integrity of Social Security and Medicare

Also supporting the legislation were numerous taxpayer protection groups such as Americans for Tax Reform and Citizens for a Sound Economy, business coalitions such as the Small Business Survival Committee and the National Federation of Independent Businesses, and numerous organizations representing working families.

On June 17, 1998, the Tax Code Termination Act made history, passing the U.S. House of Representatives by 219 to 209, stunning critics and supporters alike. Though it would later get bottled up in the Senate, a new marker had been set down in the long march toward tax freedom.

"Today's victory is one small step for Congress, one giant leap for the American taxpayer," I told the media. "Think about how far this effort has come in just three years. This is no longer a one-man crusade against high taxes and IRS corruption. It's become a national movement, and it's gaining momentum." Indeed it has.

When our Founding Fathers signed the Declaration of Independence, they pledged their lives, their fortunes, and their sacred honor to fight successfully against King George's reign of tax terror. Teddy Roosevelt bolted the Republican Party to form the "Bull Moose Party" to oppose massive, new anti-growth tariffs imposed by his fellow Republicans. John Kennedy squared off against establishmentarians for across-the-board tax cuts to "get America moving again." Ronald Reagan battled the Washington establishment to win bold, dramatic tax relief for the American people.

Now the time has come for another such fight over the direction of the country, and the direction of the Republican Party. Now the time has come, once and for all, to tear down this tax code.

CHAPTER SIX

PATIENT POWER

WHILE I WAS working on this book, I had the opportunity to spend some time in New Hampshire with a wonderful couple trying to raise their three kids, run their family fish market, and make ends meet. They are part of the "forgotten middle class" that was supposed to be rescued by the current administration. But they remain forgotten. Despite all of their hard work and self-sacrifice, they cannot afford health insurance for themselves or their kids. So they live from day to day and week to week with the ever-present anxiety that one of them will suffer from a major accident or illness. Everything they have worked for could be wiped away. As far as I'm concerned, as long as they live in fear, they are not free—and that is unacceptable.

We had not met to talk about health care. We had met together on April 15 to assail the IRS and talk about a new birth of tax freedom. But as we spent time together, they discovered that under my flat tax proposal they would save about $6,000. What would they do with the money? "What else?" they told me. "Get ourselves some health insurance."

Cutting and simplifying taxes would give a whole lot of working families the ability to buy themselves health insurance. But the problems facing our health care system will not be solved by tax reform alone. We must do more.

THE MIRACLE OF MODERN MEDICINE

Americans today have the best trained doctors and nurses, the highest quality medical schools, and the most advanced lifesaving technology the world has ever seen. The breakthroughs in medicine in this century have been absolutely breathtaking. But the advances in this decade alone stagger the mind: lasers… digital imaging… incredibly vivid sonograms… neonatal surgery… genetic mapping… wonder drugs—the likes of which our parents and grandparents could never have imagined.

The fact is we have the greatest health care professionals in the world. But the system they work in has serious problems that could slow or damage incredible upcoming advances and could harm the delivery of health care to the American people. Medicare is going bankrupt. Medicaid is a mess. Washington has made a hash of Medical Savings Accounts. And if all that weren't enough, Washington politicians keep talking about passing a so-called "Patient's Bill of Rights," which begs the question: Why does it take an act of Congress for patients to have flexibility and choice in what doctors they see?

The Nemours Cardiac Center at the Alfred I. duPont Hospital for Children in Wilmington, Delaware, vividly demonstrates what dedicated leadership in medicine can achieve. The center's mission is state-of-the-art reconstructive heart surgery for babies and very young children. There is hardly a form of congenital heart disease that its surgeons cannot treat effectively. But, thanks to managed care and ever-growing government intrusion, we are creating an environment increasingly hostile to initially expensive innovations.

The Nemours Cardiac Center's creator and director is Dr. William Norwood, a trailblazer in the development of reconstructive heart surgery. Norwood had always dreamed of bringing together an extraordinary team of cardiologists, anesthesiologists, surgeons, nurses, and technicians to innovatively tackle critical heart problems in newborns and young children. At other hospitals, Norwood had run into the usual roadblocks and challenges that surface when several areas of health care are competing for resources. He had even set up a specialized heart institute for children in Switzerland, but was increasingly undermined by Swiss restrictions on hiring foreign personnel. Then Norwood received a farsighted offer from the Nemours Foundation. He was asked to set up a world-class center at the duPont Hospital, with his group separate from the rest of the hospital.

Norwood is accustomed to going against the conventional wisdom when creating brilliant, new surgical techniques. For years convention had it that you shouldn't operate on babies with congenital heart problems until they were older—unless, of course, the condition was immediately life-threatening. But Norwood believes that the sooner you operate on the baby, the better the odds are that the "heart muscle will work with normal efficiency."

In 1997 I visited the center with Pete du Pont, the former governor of Delaware, and Congressman Mike Castle. We saw babies who had successfully undergone the most complicated kinds of surgery. The recuperative power of these infants was a wonder to behold.

Norwood is acutely aware of the role environment plays in the patient's recovery. The center is family-oriented, providing a private sitting room and bedroom for parents and patients to use during the child's hospital stay. Treatment areas are conveniently located on the same floor. And, if possible, when it's time for surgery, the patient's sibling or siblings take the patient to the operating room in a large red wagon filled with his or her toys. Each family has what is, in effect, a concierge. About one-third of the center's patients are from overseas, and the concierge handles everything from travel logistics to translators. For Americans, the concierge also copes with filling out and filing insurance claims.

Because of the way our health care system works today—with emphasis on restricting immediate costs—this cardiac center, despite Norwood's brilliant successes, could never happen without the Nemours Foundation. Innovations initially can be very expensive—especially when they involve equipment or procedures not listed in an insurer's handbook. The more commonplace an innovation becomes, the less expensive it is. But the ethos regarding a center like this would be: That's very nice, very moving, but it costs too much. Norwood, however, believes that if you go for quality from the outset, lower costs and efficiencies will follow. He's right, of course. But with some remarkable exceptions—like this one in Delaware—that is not how our current system works.

THE MESS OF MODERN HEALTH INSURANCE

The core problem in American health care is how we finance it, which in turn affects its delivery. As you know, most people with private health insurance get their coverage through their employers. The employer is in charge of the health care money, and many employees see health insurance as a free "perk." But the money going to buy that health insurance is part of the worker's income. The cost of the health insurance is hidden, though, because it is tax free for the worker as long as the employer buys the policy.

The real cure for what ails our health care system today is less government and more freedom.

Problems arise because the consumer isn't in charge of the money or the choices. Because he doesn't have much, if any, control over the money that is spent on his health insurance or medical care, he doesn't treat it as his own. If he saves money, he doesn't get to keep it. If he's wasteful, he doesn't get charged. Imagine if employers covered an employee's car insurance and paid for gasoline, car washes, oil changes, and all kinds of other routine maintenance—as well as traditional coverage for accidents, fire, and theft. Imagine how expensive such insurance would be. Well, in a sense, that's what's happening with health care.

Except that it's worse than that. Many workers who have health insurance that covers the bulk of their routine medical expenses fear that if they face a truly major illness or accident, they may be denied or be hindered from getting proper care. Or, almost as frightening, they fear they will find themselves financially destitute—even bankrupt—in the process of getting good care. And for those Americans who have no health insurance at all, their fears are even more intense. We have a real crisis of confidence in our health care system today.

We need a new "Health Care Declaration of Independence" that takes power out of the hands of the government and puts it back in the hands of individuals and families, where it belongs.

Now think about this question for a moment: Where else in our economy do we consider growing demand a crisis? When demand rises for cars, we applaud it. When demand for housing grows, we cheer. When demand for microchips and software grows, the markets go crazy. So why is the growing demand for health care considered a crisis? Precisely because of the horrible way we finance it.

In fact, when you think about it, we don't even have real health care insurance. We have a system where employers prepay an estimate of next year's health care costs for their employee. So not surprisingly, we have a system that creates incentives for insurance companies to avoid people with illnesses, or deny sick people the amount and quality coverage they may really need in order to keep costs down. Instead of shared risk—the traditional basis of insurance—we have risk avoidance.

What, then, do we do now? Some believe more government is the answer. But government isn't the answer; it's the problem. Who do you think created this convoluted health care financing system in the first place? The federal government. Back during World War II,

Washington imposed wage and price controls. But employers needed to attract good people. So they created a back door fringe benefits deduction to allow employees to get their health insurance on the job tax free. It was a way of giving people a pay raise without violating wage controls. That put us on the road to where we are today.

All Americans should be free to choose doctors they trust, specialists they need, and second opinions they want for themselves, their children, and their families.

But it didn't stop there. Today, the Washington politicians get all upset about rising costs and the growing number of uninsured. So what do they do? They pile on all kinds of new rules and regulations. But these just drive up the cost of health care and increase the ranks of the uninsured. People get more upset. So the politicians pass more rules. And the vicious, counterproductive cycle goes on and on and on. That's what the Clinton-Gore administration's health care plan was all about in 1994, and that's what the so-called Patient's Bill of Rights is all about today.

A NEW HEALTH CARE
DECLARATION OF INDEPENDENCE

The truth is that the real cure for what ails our health care system is less government and more freedom.

I believe that what is needed is a "Health Care Declaration of Independence"—an entirely new approach to health care that takes power out of the hands of the government, the "gatekeepers," and other third-party payers, and puts it back in the hands of individuals and families, where it belongs. Indeed, there are some core values that ought to guide the American health care system as we go into the twenty-first century.

First, all Americans should be free to choose doctors they trust, specialists they need, and second opinions they want for themselves, their children, and their families. It is absolutely critical that we work

together to fully restore and protect the doctor-patient relationship—because it is the heart and the soul of a truly compassionate
and effective health care system.

*Second, all Americans should be free from the fear of being left behind in
this Information Age economy without real health security.* Today, forty-
three million Americans have no coverage. That is growing by more
than a million people every year. In California alone, seven million
people have no health insurance—that's growing by thousands of
people every month. Hortensia Magana, a Latino business leader,
wrote a commentary in the *Los Angeles Times* in which she said, "If
members of Congress and the growing list of presidential candidates want to meet the Latino community's most pressing need, the
issue they will deal with immediately is health care." She noted that
38 percent of non-elderly Latinos in California have no health insurance. "Latinos are getting the short end of the health care stick," she
said. She's right, and she's not alone… and that's not good enough.
Not in America as we enter the twenty-first century.

*Third, all Americans should be free to purchase affordable, portable,
private health insurance for themselves and their families.* They should
be free to buy affordable catastrophic health insurance policies that
they own, that cannot be taken away from them, and that gives them
real peace of mind by truly protecting them in case of a major illness
or accident. No American should be forced
into government-run health care programs
or forced into top-down—and sometimes
heavy-handed—managed care and HMO
programs against their will. If people are
happy with their HMOs, that's fine. But they
should have real catastrophic coverage and be
free to choose from a variety of other insurance options.

**All Americans should
be free to purchase
affordable, portable,
private health insur-
ance for themselves
and their families.**

*Fourth, health care providers and insurers should also be free and
encouraged to create a vibrant, dynamic private health insurance market that meets the needs of real customers, that responds to the dissatis-*

factions in the marketplace, and that treats people with dignity and respect. That's how we restore confidence, improve quality, achieve more medical breakthroughs, and control costs—through the miracle of the marketplace and the healing power of competition.

Fifth, all American workers should be free to know how much their employers are spending on their health care, and all Americans should be free to make their own health care spending decisions. They should be free to use Medical Savings Accounts (MSAs) if they want to. MSAs work like Individual Retirement Accounts. An employer or worker or both should be free to deposit money into the MSA. MSAs also give people the freedom to choose doctors they trust.

No American should be forced into government-run health care programs or forced into managed care and HMO programs against their will.

Certainly no one should be forced to use MSAs. But they are good products. They work in the real world for real people, and every American should have access to them.

Now, these are some core values that can help us put patients first. The question, of course, is: How do we put these values into practice?

As we go into the twenty-first century, we need to begin moving toward a system that allows people the freedom to buy low-cost, high-deductible catastrophic health insurance coverage to protect themselves in the event of a major illness or accident. A catastrophic policy for a single person might have a deductible of, say, $1,500 a year. A family's deductible might be $2,000 a year. Once those deductibles are met, the catastrophic insurance policies would provide 100 percent coverage from that point forward. Such plans cost less than traditional insurance coverage because they do not cover routine health care expenses. Instead, they give people real peace of mind that they can get the treatment they need and will not be wiped out financially if the unthinkable happens and they start running up massive medical bills.

MEDICAL SAVINGS ACCOUNTS—
SECURITY AND CHOICE

At the same time, we should also make it easier for people to open tax-free MSAs to cover routine medical expenses and meet their deductibles.

In 1996 Congress created an MSA pilot program. That was the good news. The bad news was they put MSAs in a regulatory straightjacket which we should now remove. We should allow anyone to buy them—not just the self-employed and companies with fewer than fifty employees, like federal law currently demands. We should stop Washington from imposing artificially high deductibles of $3,000 to $4,500 for working families. That is pricing many people out of the market. Instead, we should let the markets set the deductibles so people can really afford these policies. We should also let contributions to MSAs equal 100 percent of the deductible. And we should remove the cap on the number of MSAs that can be sold. Today, Washington limits total tax-free MSAs to a ridiculously low 750,000 policies. But that is only discouraging many insurance companies from truly developing this important market. That must be changed.

Right now, there is growing bipartisan Congressional support to expand access to MSAs and to repeal their regulatory limitations. We should move aggressively on this front.

But what is really amazing about MSAs is that they're helping people most in need of real health security even though Washington has created this regulatory straightjacket. According to the Treasury Department, *one-third of all new MSA policyholders are people who were previously uninsured.* According to Golden Rule Insurance— the largest provider of MSAs in the country—75 percent of new MSA buyers are working families, 77 percent are self-employed, and 10 percent are single parents. These are the people we want to help, and MSAs are helping us get the job done.

The Clinton-Gore administration calls MSAs a "poison pill." That is easy for politicians to say when they already have good health insurance and the freedom to choose doctors they trust. But what about Melanie Horkman, a single mom in Green Bay, Wisconsin, who had no health insurance at all for four years until she was able to buy an MSA? What about Ben Harmon, a self-employed contractor in St. John's, Michigan, and his wife, Carmen, and their two young children? They didn't have any health care insurance either until MSAs became available. What about the millions of families just like these two that could really benefit from MSAs?

TAKING A CUE FROM THE PRIVATE SECTOR

One of the reasons I'm such a big believer in putting patients back in charge of their own health care spending decisions is my experience as a CEO. When I took the helm of *Forbes* magazine in 1990, we were experiencing double-digit annual health premium increases. It was unsustainable. The question I asked was obvious: How do we get our people to treat the health care money we spend on their behalf as if it were their own money?

The question suggested the answer. We put in a variation of MSAs. We give our people $1,500 a year to spend on routine health expenses. The more money they save, the more they get to keep—and it works. People now understand that being a wise shopper has a direct benefit to their own bottom line. Our expenses are no higher today per person than they were seven years ago—and none of our people has been forced into programs that restrict their choice of doctors. In fact, each year over 40 percent of our people receive bonus checks for the unused amount of money in their health care accounts.

There are other ways to give people more control over their own money. For example, we need to reform flexible health care spending accounts. Known as Section 125 flexible spending plans, these accounts allow workers to divert a certain amount from their paychecks tax free to be used for medical and other expenses. The problem today is that if the money allocated for health care isn't spent by the end of the year, the employee loses it. That's crazy. It gives people the incentive to go buy medical care they don't really need at the end of the year, just so they won't lose their own money. Why not let people roll their money over at the end of the year, and build it up with tax-free interest?

We've also got to start giving people without health insurance the freedom to buy into affordable private health care networks. We need to make it easier for churches, community organizations, professional associations, unions, and other groups to create their own networks of affordable insurance pools for people trying to buy their own coverage. Every American should be able to get the same advantages of group-purchasing that people with job-based coverage currently get.

We've also got to dramatically reduce the regulations, mandates, and price controls that are driving up the cost of health insurance and increasing the ranks of the uninsured. Let me cite one example. Between 1990 and 1994 sixteen states aggressively passed laws to help improve access to health coverage. I'm sure this was all done with the best of motives. The problem is, it backfired. By 1996 these sixteen states were seeing their uninsured populations increasing *eight times faster* than the other thirty-four states. Why? Because all these new rules and regulations imposed new costs on health insurers. That drove insurance prices up. And *that* caused some small business owners to drop coverage since they couldn't afford the higher premiums. It caused more working people to drop coverage for themselves and their children, and it kept many uninsured people priced out of the marketplace altogether.

This is a classic case of the unintended consequences of government regulation, and we've got to reverse this trend. We need to create a health insurance system that gives people the freedom to choose from a number of options. Americans should be free to buy basic, catastrophic coverage they can afford. They should also be free to buy more expensive and comprehensive coverage if that's what they want. But we can't keep allowing federal and state governments to impose top-down rules and regulations that end up causing more harm than good.

What if every employer in America actually told workers—in plain English, right on their pay stub, without any gobbledy-gook—precisely how much their health insurance costs? I think that would stun most workers. Don't you think workers at, say, General Motors would like to know how much their employers are spending on their health insurance every year? After all, General Motors spends more each year on health care than on buying steel to build its cars and trucks. Healthy markets require educated consumers. And as we move toward a vibrant, dynamic, competitive health care system in the twenty-first century, we need to help people understand the full cost of the health care they are using.

If we make the reforms outlined here, I believe that we'll begin to see the cost of health coverage come down dramatically, and access to affordable health coverage will expand dramatically. That's where we want to go, because health insurance that costs less not only helps people who already have job-based insurance, it will also truly help those who don't have any health insurance at all. In fact, I believe that we can reduce the number of uninsured Americans by one-third to one-half by removing the regulatory straightjacket on the health care industry and by creating a truly dynamic and competitive market that allows people to own their own health insurance that they can take with them, even if they move, change jobs, or start their own businesses. That would be a huge leap forward.

RESCUING MEDICARE AND MEDICAID

Finally, there is the whole issue of Medicare and Medicaid. It is absolutely imperative that we rescue these two programs because they are designed to help our most vulnerable citizens. The people who depend upon Medicare are our parents and grandparents. Those with limited financial means rely on Medicaid.

Today we have about forty million Americans on Medicare. We are spending an average of $6,000 a year on each beneficiary. The system is in serious trouble. The lives of real Americans are hanging in the balance. Yet some just want to play election year political games with the health security of the elderly. They want to scare people. I think that's wrong.

We need to strengthen Medicare by taking money and power and control out of the hands of the government bureaucrats and putting it into the hands of beneficiaries, where it belongs. Seniors should have access to a wide variety of health care options, just like government workers do in the Federal Employees Health Benefits Program. One option should be Medicare MSAs. That means getting rid of the cap which right now permits only 390,000 such policies. That's crazy. Every senior should be free to choose a Medicare MSA—because MSAs work. They provide real catastrophic insurance. No one would then need to buy Medigap insurance—which 70 percent of all Medicare beneficiaries now buy, and which costs them about $1,200 a year. And, of course, Medicare MSAs give seniors the freedom to choose their own doctors and hospitals. MSA money can also be used for prescription drugs and other expenses not covered by traditional Medicare.

We've also got to repeal Medicare Section 4507—a nasty provision slipped into the 1997 budget deal which effectively prohibits seniors from privately contracting with health care providers for medical services outside the government-run Medicare system. For heaven's sake, even in Britain—the mother of socialized medicine—people can opt out. Why not in America?

The bottom line is this: We absolutely must not leave our parents and grandparents trapped in a system of socialized medicine while the rest of us work to improve our health care, expand our choices, and increase our freedom. That's not America, and that's not how we should do business.

The same is true with Medicaid. Do you realize that today we have about thirty-five million Americans on Medicaid? We spend an average of $4,000 a year on each recipient. What do they get for that money? They're trapped in a demeaning, highly bureaucratic, and essentially socialized medical system. Is that the best we can do? Not likely.

We must not leave our parents and grandparents trapped in a system of socialized medicine while the rest of us work to improve our health care, expand our choices, and increase our freedom.

How, then, do we empower people on Medicaid? How can we give them the freedom to shop for real private health insurance from a variety of options, including catastrophic coverage and MSAs, or buying into networks like the Federal Employees Health Benefits Program and HealthMarts? There has been some progress here. We're seeing states use waivers to allow Medicaid recipients to use HMOs and managed care programs.

But we really need to keep thinking about how to give people more freedom and more incentives to shop wisely for their own health care and practice preventive medicine. One idea to be looked at is how to convert the money that federal and state governments spend on each Medicaid beneficiary into individual "medical coupons" that would allow them to go into the private insurance market and buy real coverage.

THE ROAD TO FREEDOM

The truth is that there are really two roads we can take as we face these issues. Some would have us go down the road to health care completely run by the government, where bureaucrats micromanage every facet of the doctor-patient relationship and taxpayers foot every bill. The problem, as the late Nobel Prize–winning free-market economist Frederick Hayek observed, is that is the road to serfdom, not progress.

The alternative is the road to freedom—the road to a vibrant, dynamic, competitive health care system that gives people real choices, real control, and real health security. We need a system where a mother knows she is free to choose a doctor she trusts, specialists she needs, and second opinions she wants for herself, her husband, and her children. Positive change must be driven by consumers and the marketplace, not by the Washington politicians. After all, people's physical health should not come at the expense of their financial health.

CHAPTER SEVEN

SAVING SOCIAL SECURITY

HIGH ANXIETY. That may be the best way to describe how many Americans feel about their retirement as we head into the twenty-first century. I see it wherever I go.

Tens of millions of baby boomers see retirement hurtling toward them and are growing very anxious about their future. They are getting crushed by sky-high Social Security taxes. They know that the government-run retirement system is giving them a terrible return on their money. They see the stock market booming, but because of all the high taxes they are paying, many find it difficult if not impossible to scrape together enough money to really sock away in their own savings account, much less in their own Individual Retirement Account (IRA) or a 401(k) plan. And while some Americans have generous pension plans—like the cashier at Wal-Mart we learned about in Chapter 3—many work for small companies, or for themselves, and are part of no private pension system at all.

Seniors already on Social Security are also anxious. They have worked hard all their lives and want to enjoy their golden years. But many find themselves struggling to make ends meet on a fixed income. They find their Social Security benefits being heavily taxed.

Their benefits get drastically reduced if they go back to work and start earning significant amounts of money. And all the while, the politicians in Washington keep whispering about possible Social Security tax increases, benefit cuts, and changes in the Consumer Price Index that would reduce monthly cost-of-living increases.

One survey found that more generation Xers believe that they are likely to see a UFO than believe that they will ever see a Social Security check when they retire.

Women are also increasingly concerned. For one thing, they tend to live longer than men and thus are more dependent on a strong retirement security system. They can find themselves at serious economic risk if they get separated or divorced and their spouse tries to hide or deny them assets to which they are entitled. Also, only about one in five retired American women currently receives a public or private pension, and the average pension is worth only about half as much as pensions received by men.

Minorities are also worried about their retirement security. The life expectancy of an African American man born today, for example, is just 65.8 years. That means that he may very well pass away before he ever really benefits from a lifetime of his own hard work and crushing Social Security tax payments. Moreover, the vast majority of African American families own no stocks or pension funds, thus locking them out of the enormous personal wealth being created in the markets today.

Young people are also growing apprehensive. They, too, are getting hammered by high Social Security taxes. But most do not believe that they will *ever* get anything back from the government-controlled system. In fact, one survey taken in the early 1990s found that more generation Xers believe that they are likely to see a UFO (46 percent) than believe that they will ever see a Social Security check when they retire (28 percent).

With all this anxiety out there, what ever happened to Washington's pledge to "save Social Security"?

The president, vice president, and leaders of both major parties in Congress keep saying they understand that the system provides a poor return on people's money. That is true. From 1900 to 1995, the average real rate of return on stocks in the U.S. was 7.58 percent a year. By contrast, Social Security's real rate of return for an average American family is a mere 0.64 percent a year. The Washington politicians keep saying they understand the system is headed for the financial rocks. That is also true. By around 2014, Social Security will start paying out in benefits more than it is taking in through payroll taxes. They also keep saying that they will work together to avert a disaster and to protect seniors. But year after year goes by and nothing positive ever gets done.

There are plenty of misguided ideas out there. Some, for example, want government bureaucrats to invest your money in the stock market without your having any say whatsoever. But a government takeover of the stock market is not the way to save Social Security. In fact, it's the most blatant big government power grab since the Clinton-Gore administration's health care plan of 1994, which would have forced all of us into government-run HMOs. So that's a non-starter. (What do they put in the water in our nation's capital? Where is the Environmental Protection Agency when you *really* need it?)

I believe that we can do better.

THE MIRACLE OF THE MARKET

Every American should be free to participate in this new era of prosperity. That is why in the early 1980s I began suggesting that we give people the freedom to invest part and eventually the bulk of their Social Security payroll taxes in their own IRAs. It would be good for American workers and good for the economy. In my "Fact and Comment" column in *Forbes* on May 21, 1984, I wrote:

> Social Security's long-term finances are… a disaster. The post–World War II baby boomers could find the system

broke by the time they try to collect from it thirty years from now. The problem will be demographic: too many people collecting, not enough working. In addition, the way Social Security is financed is particularly destructive. High payroll taxes hurt job creation.... Unlike a normal pension scheme, Social Security does not generate capital for the private sector....

One sensible reform would let a portion of the Social Security tax be invested in Individual Retirement Accounts. Such a change might cost Uncle Sam revenues initially, but would provide a sound basis for paying beneficiaries into the next century. IRAs are fantastic generators of capital. Sadly, the budget debate is dominated by tunnel vision, by a penny-wise, pound-foolish mentality. Changes that would benefit the economy's capacity to grow but might temporarily reduce Washington's revenue, such as reducing income tax rates or truly reforming Social Security, are dismissed.

Since then I have continued writing and speaking about strengthening Social Security and IRAs. I have met with elected officials and encouraged them to pick up this banner and run with it. Yet few have seemed to understand what I've been talking about.

So when I ran for president in 1996, I set out to begin a national conversation about how to save Social Security and help turn every American worker into an owner, a real player in the free market system, not a pawn. Even some of my advisers begged me not to. *Don't you know you'll be grabbing hold of the "third rail" of American politics?* they implored. *Touch it and you die!* The Republican establishment wasn't really happy about it either. They had no positive solutions of their own, and they were terrified of incurring the wrath of the Democratic-controlled White House.

But you know what? I found that real people in the real world were interested in straight talk about big ideas. That was certainly the case in Arizona and Delaware, where I won upset primary victories against the established front-runners. Yes, the ideas I was talking about were new and innovative. Yes, they were different from the same old tired beltway blather. But that's OK. The American people are much smarter than the Washington politicians and media give them credit for.

When I ran for President in 1996, I set out to begin a national conversation about how to save Social Security.

Wherever I go, I find seniors very eager to talk about specific and practical ways of protecting their retirement security from the greedy hand of government. Likewise, baby boomers and gen-Xers are also excited by the idea of having the freedom to save and invest their own Social Security taxes in a way that allows them to create real "family capital," the kind of personal wealth that can lift millions of Americans out of poverty and can never be taken away. When I spoke to three thousand black men at a church pastored by Bishop Eddie Lee Long outside of Atlanta in March of 1999, I repeatedly received standing ovations when I talked about phasing in a system of personal retirement accounts that are real private property, cannot be taken away by the government, and can eventually be passed on to one's children and grandchildren.

That's why I'm an optimist. I think we really can save Social Security—not just talk about it—as long as we don't let ourselves be road-blocked by the political establishment.

Here's how:

FIVE STEPS TO SAVING SOCIAL SECURITY

First, we must fully protect the current Social Security system for those on it and those going on it in the next ten to fifteen years. Millions of Americans have made retirement decisions based on the contract of the current system. They should be protected. That means no benefit cuts, no tax increases, and no political monkeying with the Consumer Price Index. Promises made should be promises kept.

Second, we must stop taxing seniors' Social Security benefits and end the Social Security earnings penalty. Most Americans would be shocked to learn that up to 85 percent of the benefits seniors receive from Social Security can be taxed by Washington. If seniors want to continue working to earn additional income, their Social Security benefits may be reduced dramatically, depending on how much they earn from working. How can this possibly be considered good public policy? These are our parents and grandparents we are talking about. Why are we letting Washington tax the very benefits they have worked a lifetime to accumulate? Why are we imposing on them top marginal rates that can reach over 80 percent if they want to keep working to make ends meet? It's crazy. More than that, it's immoral. Such taxes should be abolished. It is time we started honoring and valuing the enormous contribution seniors make to our families, our communities, and our economy.

We can save Social Security—not just talk about it—as long as we don't let ourselves be road-blocked by the political establishment.

Third, we should use the Social Security surplus to help phase in a new Social Security system of personal retirement accounts for younger workers. Let's give people the freedom to choose to stay in the current system, or to invest part—and eventually the bulk—of their Social Security taxes in their own personal retirement accounts, similar to IRAs and 401(k) plans. This would give people the opportunity to take their money out of the hands of the Washington politicians and invest it in the real American economy. That way, they would retire with far more than they ever could receive under the current system.

Fourth, we must stop Washington from raiding the Social Security Trust Fund by taking the Trust Fund off-budget—out of the hands of the Washington politicians. If the board members of a major corporation were found raiding their employees' pension fund, they could be sent to jail. Yet this happens in Washington every single day. Roughly $80 billion a year in Social Security surpluses are looted from the Trust Fund to finance more wasteful, big government spending and to cover the federal government's operating budget deficit. In 2000, the Social Security surplus alone may be about $138 billion. Over the next ten years, the Social Security surplus could total about $1.8 trillion, according to the Congressional Budget Office.

Do we really want to let Washington waste all this money? Absolutely not. This is wrong, and we must bring a stop to it. Taking the Trust Fund off-budget would be helpful. But far more lastingly and substantively, the most important thing we can do is to use these surpluses to help phase in this new system of personal retirement accounts. That way, Washington politicians won't even have the opportunity to play games with all this money. It will all be in people's personal retirement accounts and thus private property that the government cannot take away.

Fifth, we must start right away, while we still have time. Today, Social Security is generating huge surpluses. But around 2014—unless serious reforms are made—the federal government will begin paying out in benefits more than it takes in through payroll taxes. Why? Because some eighty million baby boomers will begin retiring and there won't be enough young people working to pay for them all. In 1950 the payroll taxes of thirteen workers supported each Social Security recipient. Today, that number is down to just three workers. Early in the next century, the ratio will fall to just two to one. That's unsustainable. Payroll tax rates have already soared six fold over the past fifty years, from 2 percent to 12.4 percent. The amount of income subject to the tax has increased nine fold, from less than $8,000 as late as 1971 to over $72,000 today. Some 70 percent of American workers now pay more in federal payroll taxes than they do in federal income taxes. Such a punishing tax burden makes it almost impossible for working families to save adequately for retirement.

That is why we should begin using current Social Security surpluses to help phase in a stronger and more secure system. Federal Reserve Board Chairman Alan Greenspan has testified to Congress that the sooner we start the transition to a new system, the easier such a transition will be. He is right.

PERSONAL RETIREMENT ACCOUNTS
WORK AROUND THE WORLD

Other countries have made successful transitions to personal retirement accounts. Great Britain did, for example, with the help of Margaret Thatcher. More than 73 percent of eligible British workers have chosen to invest their payroll taxes in private stocks and equities. As a result, British workers have averaged a 13 percent return on their private investments, and Britain's pension pool, now worth over U.S. $1 trillion, is larger than the pension funds of all other European countries combined.

Chile has also created a system of personal retirement accounts and financed the transition without tax increases and without benefit cuts. It also eased people's concerns by giving people the freedom to choose between the new system and the old. One out of four eligible Chilean workers chose the new system in the first month alone. Today, more than 95 percent of eligible Chilean workers participate in the new system.

José Piñera was the architect of Chile's inspiring effort to save Social Security. As he puts it: "The new pension system gives Chileans a personal stake in the economy. A typical Chilean worker is not indifferent to the stock market or interest rates. When workers feel that they own a part of the country, not through party bosses or a Politburo, they are much more attached to the free market and a free society."

Isn't this what we want, too, every American having a stake in our free society? Absolutely.

HOW WOULD THE NEW SYSTEM WORK?

Here's how the system could work in the U.S.:

- You would be free to choose to stay in the current system, or invest part—and eventually the lion's share—of your Social Security payroll taxes in your own personal retirement account, similar to an IRA or 401(k) plan.

- You would own this account—not the government. It couldn't be taken away from you. In your will, you could leave your assets to your spouse, children, relatives, or even your favorite charities.

- Married couples would share benefits equally. Half your money would go into your own account, and half would go into your spouse's account. In the case of separation or divorce, you would not have to go to court to fight over the assets. They would already be yours.

- A small portion of your money would go to purchase your own private disability insurance and life insurance. Again, you would own these insurance policies—not the government.

- You would be free to choose which investment company to use. You would also be free to change investment companies. All companies would be licensed by the Securities and Exchange Commission. We must absolutely make sure this system is safe and secure.

- You would be free to choose what investment options you prefer from a menu of sound fiscal choices. The menu could include stock index funds, mutual funds, U.S. Treasury bonds, other forms of bonds, and bank certificates of deposit. You would be free to change investment options as you see fit. Some basic guidelines would be established to protect your economic security. Obviously, investing in Honduran race horses or Asian derivatives is not going to be part of this new system.

- You would receive a periodic printed statement detailing the performance in your account. In fact, in this Internet Age, we could also create the ability for you to check the status of your account on-line—any time of the day or night—with your own secure password.

- You would be free to choose your own retirement age, rather than have it be mandated from Washington. You could work with a financial planner to figure out how much money you would like to retire on, set your own personal goals, and know that all your hard work was really building toward something special.

- The assets you build up in your personal retirement account would not be subject to federal income tax. The federal tax on capital gains would be eliminated to help maximize the return on your money. The "death" tax would be abolished so you could pass on your assets to your spouse or children without suffering financially. Most people do not realize that under current law, your Individual Retirement Account can be taxed at rates upwards of 85 percent. How is this possible? Say you have an IRA and then you pass away. The IRA then becomes subject to estate taxes that can run as high as 55 percent. Then, when your children try to withdraw the money in the IRA, it is subject to personal income taxes. All that nonsense would disappear under this new plan.

- Undergirding the entire system would be the assurance that the federal government would guarantee you a minimum benefit. A safety net is absolutely essential. If the stock market crashes—or if for some other reason the money in your account when you retire does not meet the guaranteed minimum—the federal government would make up the difference.

NO ONE IS LEFT BEHIND

What difference would a new Social Security system like this make in the lives of an average working family? In their book *Common*

Cents, Common Dreams, authors Peter J. Ferrara and Michael D. Tanner consider a married couple where the husband is a construction worker earning $36,000 a year and the wife does not work outside the home. If this couple were free to invest their payroll taxes in a personal retirement account and chose a conservative mixed stock and bond mutual fund with an average 7 percent real rate of return (after inflation) each year, they could retire with a lump sum of about $700,000, in 1997 dollars. If they chose a solely stock mutual fund, they could retire with over $1 million in their account. With that, they could buy an annuity guaranteeing them an annual income of more than $100,000, nearly three times what they currently earn.

IS THIS POSSIBLE?

This is all possible because the private American economy provides a far greater return on people's money than the government can. Over the past seventy years, stocks on the New York Stock Exchange have provided an average 7 percent real rate of return every year, while corporate bonds have provided an average 3 percent real rate of return every year. This is the magic of a free society.

The Washington political culture has a difficult time understanding all this because it is locked in a static, zero-sum mindset and does not get the dynamics of growth and freedom. In politics, life is zero sum. You are either up or down. There is no way two people can benefit at the same time. Think about it. Either you win the election or you lose. Either you get the coveted committee assignment or you do not. But in the real world, life is not zero sum. One person's gain does not mean another person's loss. Everyone can move ahead if he is helping meet the needs and wants of others.

Saving Social Security, then, is not a matter of taking something away from one group of people in order to help another group of people. It is a matter of letting every American benefit from a strong and growing economy. In fact, by increasing the rate of savings and investment in America, moving to a system of personal retirement accounts will grow the economy even more. That, in turn, will increase family incomes, create more and better-paying jobs, and provide the government with enough resources to meet its other obligations. Some economists believe a fully funded system of personal retirement accounts would help create a million new jobs, increase an average family of four's income by some $5,000 a year, and increase the nation's total wealth by $10 trillion to $20 trillion. The real danger is not in moving toward such a system. The *real* danger is in delay.

The good news is that support for personal retirement accounts has grown dramatically in recent years. Part of the reason, I believe, is the vigorous and consistent advocacy by a wide variety of people and organizations all across the country. One such advocate is Sam Beard, a lifelong Democrat, who has been urging his party to embrace personal retirement accounts as a way of helping low-income Americans create real wealth. "Most Americans are on a treadmill because they have but one source of income: wages," wrote Beard in a 1995 essay in *Policy Review*. "The way to get ahead is to earn income from capital. Money makes money. With capital, you can retire in comfort and bequeath a nest egg to your children." He is absolutely right.

PERSONAL FREEDOM AND ECONOMIC SECURITY

But even more important than all the advocacy has been a dramatic paradigm shift over the past two decades from faith in big government to faith in personal freedom and the long-term economic security afforded by having a stake in the free market. In a whole variety of ways, Americans have simply grown more and more comfortable with how they can benefit from market solutions, and more and more uncomfortable with how they are being left behind by ineffective government programs.

We are seeing the rise of a new generation of investors. The percentage of Americans who now own stocks has quadrupled since the mid-1960s to more than four-in-ten adults. About 125 million Americans are now beginning to participate in the prosperity of the New Economy. And it's not the same old crowd. According to a study by the Federal Reserve, nearly half of Americans earning between $25,000 and $50,000 now own at least some stocks. Nearly half of the country's stock market investors are now women. More than half are under the age of fifty. Half have no college degree. The number of minorities participating in the stock market is also growing, though it is still far too small.

As people's comfort level with investing grows, so too does their desire to choose a free market option over the current, government-run system. Now we need to open up the system and let everyone participate. No one should be left behind.

After all, right before us is the biggest empowerment issue we have seen in years, one that will rival the GI Bill and the Homestead Act. Real Social Security reform could lead to the greatest expansion of wealth for working families that America has ever seen. What are we waiting for?

CHAPTER EIGHT

ENVIRONMENTAL STEWARDSHIP

ONE OF OUR great strengths as Americans is that we care deeply about the quality of our lives and the quality of our environment. We want to be free to enjoy time away from work with family and friends, and we want to be free to enjoy the great outdoors. That's certainly true of our family. One of the things I enjoy most is going on long bicycle trips on summer and fall weekends with our girls—away from the phones, away from the traffic, away from all the clutter of life.

One of my fondest memories of growing up was our family trips out West every summer. My mom would pack up us kids in our family station wagon and take us out to Wyoming and Colorado to play and explore and pretend we were cowboys (at least that's how I thought of it). I love my home state of New Jersey. But for me, nothing has ever quite captured the magic and mystery of this great continent as the mountains and prairies and raging rivers of the American West. I'm sure that's a large part of how I came to feel so strongly about the need to protect our environment.

As we go into a new century and a new economy, we must be mindful of the enormous responsibility we have to be good stewards of the air, land, water, and wildlife with which we have been blessed.

At the same time, we must safeguard the property rights of farmers, ranchers, families, and business owners. We must guard against the overreaching hand of big government trying to take away our freedom and with it our sense of responsibility. And we must always protect the environment in a manner consistent with our values.

ENVIRONMENTAL PROGRESS

Americans have much of which to be proud. Indeed, what is truly remarkable is the enormous progress we have made as a society in cleaning up our environment over the past several decades while increasing the standard of living for American families.

As we go into a new century we must be mindful to be good stewards of the air, land, water, and wildlife with which we have been blessed; safeguard the property rights of farmers, ranchers, families, and business owners; and guard against the overreaching hand of big government.

Critics have long charged, for example, that America's love of automobiles would lead to all kinds of environmental nightmares and diminish our quality of life. Actually, the opposite has been true. The automobile has made the American people more free—free to work and earn a living, free to roam and ramble—and in the process it has dramatically improved our quality of life.

The automobile has brought about new challenges, of course. But with new challenges have come new innovations. The American people have tackled pollution problems with their characteristic can-do attitude, and the results have been impressive. Between 1972 and 1990, for example, General Motors reduced by 44 percent the amount of energy it uses to build each of its vehicles. Delco has cut by two-thirds the amount of lead it uses in each of its car batteries. New American cars built in the 1990s emit 96 percent less carbon monoxide than those built twenty years earlier. And Honda America announced in April of 1998 a new Civic GX built in Ohio that runs on natural gas and, the company claims, is "the cleanest internal combustion car on earth."

As Americans gradually switch from older, heavily polluting cars, to newer, cleaner models, the prospects for a cleaner environment gradually improve as well. In fact, from 1990 through 1997, one innovative company known as Eco-Scrap actually bought and proceeded to junk more than 17,000 older, high–pollution-emitting cars in Southern California and Arizona. By getting these clunkers off the roads permanently, Eco-Scrap officials estimate they helped stop nineteen million pounds of pollution from being pumped into our atmosphere.

THE NEW ECONOMY IS
A CLEANER ECONOMY

Sweeping changes in the American economy are also helping reduce air pollution. As we make the transition from an old, Industrial Age economy to a new, Information Age economy, older, heavily polluting factories are gradually being replaced by newer, cleaner ones. Huge, filthy smokestacks and sewers are gradually being replaced by tiny, state-of-the-art microchips and fiber-optic cables spewing information rather than toxic waste. As our nation becomes wealthier, we are also becoming healthier, able to afford new technologies that can help us clean up the environment and keep it clean. As a result, no longer do Pittsburgh-area children have to go to school with handkerchiefs over their noses and mouths to keep out all the smoke and soot as they did fifty years ago. No longer do train passengers have to inhale thick, black smoke from coal-burning engines as they once did.

In this age of dramatic economic change, innovative new technologies, a greater awareness of the problems caused by industrial pollution, and some real cooperation between the private sector and government, we have had remarkable success in improving our environment. Between 1970 and 1995, for example, total emissions of six major air pollutants—carbon monoxide, lead, nitrogen dioxide, ozone, particulate matter, and sulfur dioxide—decreased by 31 percent, according to a report by the Environmental Protection Agency (EPA). And this was despite the fact that during the same time the U.S. population increased, the gross domestic product increased, and there were millions more cars and trucks on the road. Regulation played a role in these improvements, of course, but so did the ingenuity of the private sector.

TECHNOLOGY FOR CLEANER WATER

Water quality in America has also been steadily improving. Back in 1969, Ohio's Cuyahoga River actually caught fire because it was so heavily littered with industrial debris. Since then, much progress has been made. Wastewater treatment of industrial and municipal sewage has, according to the EPA, helped reduce the release of organic wastes by 46 percent, toxic organics by 99 percent, and toxic metals by 98 percent. A national oil recycling project with more than 7,100 collection sites in forty-seven states and the District of Columbia has helped prevent millions of gallons of used oil from being dumped into the country's sewage system. New water purification systems are also being developed by the private sector using a wide variety of innovative and sophisticated new filtering systems and ultraviolet light treatments. As a result of these and other innovations, a study by the Association of State and Interstate Water Pollution Control Administrators found that between 1972 and 1992, over 95 percent of U.S. lakes, rivers, and streams maintained or improved in quality.

Greater public and private vigilance and new technologies are also helping us protect our environment from oil spills. We all remember the unfortunate Exxon *Valdez* accident in March of 1989, when some eleven million gallons of oil spilled into Alaska's Prince William Sound. Since then, great progress has been made in preventing similar accidents in the future. High-tech tug boats—

such as the state-of-the-art "Nanuq," built in the aftermath of the *Valdez* accident—now guide oil tankers in and out of busy ports. Instead of limited radar systems like the one that lost track of the *Valdez*, officials now use global positioning satellite systems and sophisticated new computers to track the precise movements of every tanker and tug boat and provide an early warning if trouble lies ahead. Oil cleanup crews and cutting-edge oil skimming systems that can rapidly recover hundreds of thousands of gallons of spilled oil are now in place and on alert every day in Alaska, California, and elsewhere. The result? "In the tanker industry, there have been no large oil spills since 1991, and the number of tanker spills has dropped from a high of 24.2 spills-per-year between 1970 and 1979 to 7.8 spills-per-year from 1990 to 1997," reported Alaska Congressman Don Young in April of 1999.

> **America's can-do spirit, new technologies, private stewardship, and private-public partnerships have steadily improved our environment.**

We are also doing much better at preventing leaks and spills from offshore oil rigs and the pipelines that bring oil to refineries on shore. In 1969 an offshore oil rig accident dumped some three million gallons of crude oil into the waters off the coast of Santa Barbara, California. Since then, extensive measures have been taken to prevent similar mishaps from happening. The *Los Angeles Times* reported in January of 1999 that underwater seismic tests are now conducted before drilling occurs to help officials anticipate potential geological problems. Sophisticated sensors and computers monitor every phase of the drilling process and, if necessary, can automatically trigger "blowout preventers" that pour mud and chemicals into the hole to block pressurized petroleum from surging to the surface and leaking into the water. To prevent pipeline leaks, "anti-corrosion chemicals are added and course along with the oil in the pipeline," noted reporter Gary Polakovic. "Divers and robotic submersible cameras inspect the pipes' exterior. Inside the 20-inch-diameter pipe, a big rubber ball called a 'smart pig' crawls from one end to the other in a never-ending search for leaks. Ultrasonic devices aim high-frequency sound waves at the pipe to spot minute cracks." As a result, the severity of platform and pipeline accidents have been dramatically reduced, and "83 percent of spills off the [California] coast now involve discharges of 10 gallons or less." That, too, is real progress.

HEALTHIER FORESTS

America's forests are also increasingly strong and healthy. At the beginning of the twentieth century, President Theodore Roosevelt warned Congress that "a timber famine" was "inevitable." The *New York Times* published headlines declaring "The End of the Lumber Supply" and "Supply of Wood Nears End: Much Wasted and There's No Substitute." But as we enter the twenty-first century, states like Maine, New Hampshire, Vermont, and New York that had once experienced serious forest reductions now have some twenty-six million more acres of forest than they had at the turn of the century. Nationally, we have more trees today than we had on the first Earth Day in 1970, as well as more trees than we had seventy years ago.

At the same time, we also have the world's largest forest and paper industry, employing 1.6 million Americans with annual sales of roughly a quarter of a trillion dollars. How is such a thing possible, leading the world in wood harvesting yet also having larger, healthier forests? The answer, in large part, is private property rights. Private industry is not destroying our nation's forests; it is replenishing them. American companies realize that they have a major economic incentive to plant new trees aggressively. After all, if they simply clear-cut forests, abandon them, and move on—as was done in the past—they would eventually put themselves out of business. While there have been real problems in America's forests, private landowners are showing that timber production and sound environmental stewardship can go hand in hand.

"Yes, a lot of trees have been cut down to make today's newspaper," wrote reporter John Tierney in a 1996 *New York Times* article. "But even more trees will probably be planted in their place. America's supply of timber has been increasing for decades, and the nation's forests have three times more wood today than in 1920."

In fact, most of the timber that is harvested in the United States today comes from what are known as "second-growth" forests, forests whose trees have been harvested once and were then replanted. Each year, Americans plant about 1.6 billion trees, or about six trees for every one we use. In Georgia alone—where forestry is one of the state's most important industries, employing more than 170,000 people—an average of 613,090 trees have been planted each day for the past twenty years. As a result, Georgia's forests increased by some 400,000 acres from 1989 to 1997.

North Maine Woods is a organization of individuals, families, and businesses who believe in harvesting trees, planting new ones, and always being careful to be good stewards of the environment. They maintain nearly three million acres of commercial forest land near the Canadian border. Two generations of trees have been commercially harvested there, and a third generation is now being grown. At the same time, private citizens can take advantage of two thousand miles of permanently maintained roads to go camping, fishing, hiking, and bird watching. It's a wonderful model of finding a healthy balance between community, commerce, and protecting the great outdoors.

Meanwhile, over the last several decades, the U.S. paper industry has tried to become a better environmental steward as well. It has reduced by 38 percent the amount of fossil fuel required to produce a ton of paper. The paper industry has also reduced by 90 percent its sulphur compounds emissions, which can cause such terrible odors in paper mill communities. These are also important steps in the right direction.

PROTECTING WETLANDS AND WILDLIFE

While we have worked hard to improve the health of our forests in the twentieth century, we have also worked hard to slow the loss of wetlands—swamps, marshes, and bogs that are vital wildlife habitats—since the 1950s. As a result of heightened public awareness of the importance of these areas and aggressive public and private efforts, hundreds of thousands of acres of new wetlands are now being created. Several organizations have been particularly successful in this regard. Ducks Unlimited, for example, is the world's largest private waterfowl and wetlands habitat conservation organization, with nearly one million financial contributors. Since its founding in 1937 the group has acquired nearly eight million acres of sensitive wildlife habitat in the United States, Canada, and Mexico and has worked hard to improve such land and make it a better habitat for various forms of wildlife, particularly ducks. Such efforts are paying off. With the creation of new wetlands and other important improvements, there has been a 63 percent increase in the North American duck population in the 1990s alone.

Just as cooperative efforts between private citizens, business leaders, and government officials are helping bring back America's forests and wetlands, similar efforts are helping bring back previously endangered species. The very symbol of our country—the American bald eagle—had become nearly extinct by the 1960s, largely due to the overuse of the pesticide DDT. Fewer than 450 eagle pairs were known to be living in the continental United States. With the banning of DDT in 1972, the population of this great bird once again began to flourish. Today, there are more than 5,000 known nesting pairs of bald eagles in the continental United States. In Maryland alone, scientists say there are six times more bald eagles in the state than when they started keeping records back in 1977. Finally, America's symbol is no longer endangered.

American bison—which many call buffalo—have also made a remarkable comeback. At the beginning of the twentieth century,

fewer than 1,500 bison existed in the United States, the vast majority having been killed off in the nineteenth century. Today, however, the bison population is growing by 20 percent a year, and there
are now some 250,000 bison in the United States. What happened?
Once again the answer lies in private property rights. Some bison
were saved by private conservation groups that appreciated the value
of this majestic creature. Also, enterprising ranchers discovered
that Americans love bison burgers, steaks, and stew. Bison not only
tastes good, but it is also low fat. Once people had an incentive not
only to protect the bison but also to raise them commercially, the
word "endangered" no longer applied. Even environmental enthusi-
ast Ted Turner owns a company called U.S. Bison, with herds total-
ing some 15,000 bison on ranches in the West.

This is all very good news. As a result of America's can-do spirit,
new technologies, private stewardship, and a healthy partnership
between private citizens and their elected officials, our environment has been steadily improving.

THE GOOD NEWS INDICATORS

"The environment is cleaner than at any time in the past half-
century" and the average American "is exposed to fewer potentially
harmful pollutants than at any time since the 1930s," wrote Joseph
Bast, Peter Hill, and Richard Rue of the Heartland Institute in their
1994 survey of environmental trends. "Air and water pollution,
which had risen during the 1940s and 1950s, have fallen consistently and considerably since that time. Today, pollution of all kinds
is responsible for less than one percent of cancer deaths."

The *Index of Leading Environmental Indicators*, published in April
of 1998 by the Pacific Research Institute in California, also found
strong evidence of environmental progress. "This report finds that,
contrary to public opinion, objectives for protecting human health
and the environment in most instances are being met, pollution
and wastes are being controlled, and resources and land are being

sustainably and effectively managed," wrote editors Steven Hayward and Laura Jones. "Environmental quality in both the United States and Canada is *improving*, not deteriorating." The authors noted, for example, that "forests are increasing as growth exceeds the harvesting of trees both in the United States and Canada." They also noted that air pollution "has decreased considerably," "the amounts of toxic chemicals exposed to the environment is decreasing," and "critical wetland habitat is not declining."

WHY WASHINGTON IS PART OF THE PROBLEM

Is there more to be done? Sure there is, and we need to stay focused on improving the quality of our air, land, water, and wildlife as we move into a new century and this New Economy. The question is: What's the best way to move forward? The answer is to rely less on coercive, top-down, Washington-knows-best bureaucracies and regulatory straightjackets and to rely more on an approach that is consistent with our values of individual freedom, personal responsibility, and local and community control. That means emphasizing private stewardship and property rights, market-based incentives, innovative new technologies, regulatory flexibility, sound science, commonsense risk assessment and cost-benefit analyses, and local, community-based problem-solving. But such an approach would require new leadership, because right now Washington's regulators and bureaucrats are actually making it more difficult to get the job done right.

In 1997, for example, the federal EPA issued top-down new National Ambient Air Quality Standards, despite its own assessment that air quality has improved dramatically over the past several decades. Even the White House's own Council of Economic Advisers stated that the "costs of fully complying just with the EPA's new ozone standard could reach $60 billion a year." The council also noted that "the incremental health risk reduction for more stringent standards is small, while costs are high." Officials at the White House's own Small Business Administration described the new standards as "one of the most expensive regulations faced by small businesses in ten or more years." Congressman John Dingell, the Michigan Democrat, told the press in June of 1997: "The most perverse irony is that the standards will actually delay cleaning the air in areas like Washington, D.C.... If the EPA had chosen to leave the standard unchanged, Washington would have to come into compliance by 1999. Under the new standard, the city won't have to meet the 1999 deadline and could have until 2009 or longer before being required to meet air quality standards."

In May of 1999 a federal court concluded that the EPA had overreached its constitutional authority and ignored scientific evidence suggesting that the new standards could do more harm than good. Indeed, the court found that the EPA refused to consider the threat to human health posed by its new regulations. "This court action stops the EPA from enforcing unscientifically based tougher air standards" and "signifies a positive step towards the use of sound science and risk assessment practices and a movement away from regulation by hype and fear," said Sharon Roth of the Pennsylvania Chamber of Business and Industry, one of the many local groups around the country watching the issue closely. "[T]he EPA's revised, oppressive air quality standards would be an extreme detriment to future job growth and business development in Pennsylvania."

Another example of Washington's counterproductive, top-down approach to the environment is the federal Superfund program. It was created to clean up the nation's worst hazardous waste sites. But it is a bureaucratic disaster. More than $20 billion has been spent on the program since 1980. But only 504 of the worst 1,243 sites had been cleaned up by January of 1998. The Congressional Budget Office projects that the cost of cleaning up current and future sites will run upwards of $100 billion. Cleaning up an average site can take ten to fifteen years and cost $25 million. Why? In large measure it is because the Superfund program is being run by Washington politicians and bureaucrats rather than local experts and community leaders. Much of the money, therefore, is being spent on greedy trial lawyers, reams of paperwork, and massive administrative overhead costs, rather than on actual cleanup expenses. This is leaving large numbers of "brownfields"—abandoned industrial sites waiting to be cleaned up—pockmarking American cities and scaring away businesses and much-needed inner-city jobs. The Competitive Enterprise Institute notes that in comparison to the disastrous federal program, states are doing a much better job and "Minnesota is cleaning up sites for less than $5 million each and completing cleanups in only a few years."

LOCAL PROBLEMS DESERVE
LOCAL SOLUTIONS

At the same time, suburban development and urban sprawl have become new issues for Washington politicians and federal bureaucrats. Thus we are now beginning to hear about a whole array of new, top-down federal spending and regulatory programs. But the truth is that issues of local growth and development are better handled in local communities with the help of local and state officials, not by the federal government. That's why every year *local* initiatives appear on the ballot in *local* elections. Americans don't need Washington to tell them how to plan their communities. Americans should be free to choose where they want to live, the size of their own homes, and what kind of transportation best meets their needs. They do not need Washington telling them how and where to live.

The catastrophic claims about global warming are deeply flawed. There is no real evidence that the world is heading into an age of super-heated temperatures.

Basic protections of our food, air, water, living and working conditions, and our civil rights are necessary and important. But too much red tape is counterproductive. It can suffocate small and large business, cost workers their jobs, and have minimal impact on actually protecting the environment.

LIFT THE REGULATORY BURDEN

One of the critical reasons our major industries such as steel and automobiles have long struggled to compete and succeed in the global marketplace, is a massive federal regulatory burden that acts as hidden tax, driving up costs and reducing profit margins. In 1970 the Code of Federal Regulations—the annual compilation of government decrees—filled 114 volumes. Now it fills 204 volumes and takes up nineteen feet of shelf space. This imposes a burden of somewhere between $600 billion and $700 billion a year on the American economy, or about $3,000 per year for every family in America. That is a staggering figure. But apparently it is still not enough for some politicians in Washington. They continue to propose and pass massive new regulations that rob people of their freedom and threaten to choke off America's economic expansion.

Farmers and ranchers are particularly hard hit by Washington's blizzard of red tape. "Many farmers have told me they believe their greatest obstacle to profitability is oppressive regulations which unilaterally raise production costs, and/or reduce yields," said Dean Kleckner, president of the American Farm Bureau Federation, in testimony before a congressional agriculture committee in July of 1998. "Federal regulations cost farmers and ranchers at least $20 billion of what should be net income.... Instead of working on better ways to farm, we waste creative abilities in management time on useless paperwork."

In fact, concluded Mr. Kleckner, himself a family farmer, "Overregulation has the potential to place the agricultural sector in much greater jeopardy than any bout of low prices or weather disasters."

THE KYOTO CATASTROPHE

Now comes a regulatory nightmare: an international treaty to reduce energy use and solve the so-called global warming crisis. The treaty is formally known as the Kyoto Protocol of the United Nations Framework Convention on Climate Change. The U.S. Senate voted unanimously in 1997 to oppose—in no uncertain terms—U.S. participation in the treaty if developing nations (like China, India, and Brazil) were not required to participate and if the treaty would threaten U.S. economic prosperity. But the current administration—led by its environmental point man, Vice President Al Gore—signed the treaty anyway, in defiance of the Senate.

The Kyoto Protocol is classic government overreach. For starters, it proposes a "solution" to a "problem" that very well may not exist. As Dr. S. Fred Singer, the first director of the U.S. Weather Satellite Service, has testified before Congress, "the accurate data from weather satellites available since 1979 show no increase in global average temperature and directly contradict the theoretical models and computer simulations." Dr. Singer has also noted that there is no scientific consensus that global warming is occurring and some 17,000 scientists have signed petitions against the Kyoto Protocol. The truth is that the catastrophic claims about global warming are deeply flawed. The Earth's temperatures were fluctuating long before the Industrial Revolution, and there is no real evidence that the world is heading into an age of super-heated temperatures.

Beyond the questionable science, the Kyoto treaty has other serious flaws. It leaves out more than one hundred nations (including some of the world's worst polluters). It would also have disastrous effects on the U.S. and global economies, according to numerous studies, including one conducted by the administration's own U.S. Department of Energy. This is because the treaty forces industrialized countries to reduce energy use in order to reduce their levels of net greenhouse gas emissions by 7 percent from their 1990 level. The U.S. Energy Department study estimated that complying with this treaty and achieving its goals could drive up gas prices to almost $2.00 by 2010. The cost of fuel oil could go up 76 percent. Electric prices could soar by 86 percent. Natural gas prices could skyrocket by 147 percent.

Higher energy costs would drive up the costs of everything and reduce the incomes and living standards of working families. The average American family may be forced to spend as much as 9 percent more money for groceries, 11 percent more for medical care, and 21 percent more for housing, according to various studies.

A number of economists have also found that U.S. compliance with the Kyoto treaty could cost up to 2.4 million American jobs. An analysis by the American Farm Bureau Federation found that U.S. net farm income could decrease between 24 percent and 48 percent. Also hard hit would be workers in manufacturing and energy-intensive industries, including automobiles, steel, and mining (coal miners would be particularly hammered, given the treaty's target of reducing carbon emissions). The treaty will also turn our attention away from more pressing environmental concerns, such as the millions of people in the developing world that lack access to safe drinking water and the loss of habitat for endangered species here at home and abroad. For all these reasons, the Kyoto treaty should be abandoned, not enforced. It is nothing more than another big government power grab dressed up in green.

We all want a cleaner environment for ourselves and our children. But we need not sacrifice our freedoms or economic prosperity to get there.

A NEW VISION OF
ENVIRONMENTAL STEWARDSHIP

What principles, then, should guide a new vision of environmental stewardship and personal freedom in the twenty-first century? Jonathan Adler of the Competitive Enterprise Institute and Jerry

Taylor of the CATO Institute have developed seven key principles, rooted in traditional American commonsense:

Principle One: Economic growth is a vital prerequisite for environmental progress. "A healthy economy is necessary to finance environmental improvements. Sewage treatment facilities and other environmental improvements are not free. Moreover, a significant body of literature has found a correlation between economic improvements and several measures of environmental quality. Not only are wealthier communities healthier than poor communities, on average, they tend to be more concerned about protecting environmental values." (I would add that this is one of the reasons that we need to revitalize our urban economies, so that Americans living in these low-income communities can find good jobs, raise strong families, and enjoy healthy and safe living conditions—not be left behind.)

Principle Two: The federal government should establish an environmental Hippocratic Oath: First, do no harm. "Many government programs cause or encourage environmental harm, including agricultural subsidies, corporate welfare programs, and reclamation projects. Often, this environmental harm is itself the rationale for costly environmental regulation. Before the government imposes mandates or restrictions on the private sector, it should make sure its own house is in order and eliminate environmentally destructive programs. In a similar vein, environmental policies aimed at reducing risks must not increase other risks in the process."

Principle Three: Land and natural resources are best managed by private stewards. "America has a proud conservation tradition demonstrating that private owners, whether individuals, corporations, or environmental groups, are superior land and resource managers than political entities. Rather than expanding government ownership and regulation of threatened ecological resources, policymakers should seek creative ways of expanding property-based institutions into the ecological realm."

Principle Four: State and local environmental protections should be dealt with by state and local governments. "Federalization of environmental law inevitably results in 'one-size-fits-nobody' regulations. Too often, problems that are properly handled at the local, state or regional level are handled by the federal government; most environmental concerns are local in nature, and can and should be addressed locally. There is no reason to presume that all environmental wisdom emanates from Washington, D.C. Devolution of responsibility and control will foster innovation, experimentation and encourage the development of forward-looking environmental protection strategies."

Principle Five: Remaining federal efforts should focus on results, not regulations. "Central managers can no more efficiently manage the environmental practices of thousands of commercial enterprises than they can manage dispersed economic practices. Insofar as federal regulation is necessary at all, it should establish basic environmental goals and standards in order to protect persons and their property, and allow private actors or local authorities to determine how best to achieve the stated aims."

Principle Six: No regulation without representation. "Most environmental rules are written by unelected bureaucrats in the executive branch. This undermines accountability and has encouraged excessive regulations at the expense of societal priorities. It has also impeded the development of commonsense, market-oriented approaches to environmental concerns. No lawmaking regulation should go into effect until it is affirmatively adopted by the legislature and signed into law by the executive."

Real environmental stewardship is possible in the twenty-first century, but the key is more freedom, not more government.

Principle Seven: Property owners should be compensated for regulatory takings. "It is simply unfair to require a few citizens to pay the full costs of providing public goods, environmental or otherwise. When landowners are denied the reasonable use of their land in order to advance an environmental goal, they should be compensated. This is a question of basic justice. Moreover, private property is not the enemy of environmental protection; it lies at its foundation. Requiring compensation will encourage a greater reliance on non-governmental conservation efforts, and further the cause of environmental protection."

As Americans, we feel strongly about protecting our environment, and well we should. We have been greatly blessed, and it is incumbent upon us to be good stewards of what we have been given. The question is not *whether* we should be concerned about the environment but *how* we can build upon our successes and make even greater progress. I believe that the key is finding an approach that is consistent with our values, one that relies less on the old, Soviet-style "command and control" rules that politicians so love, and more on the spirit of our new economy—individual freedom, personal responsibility, technological innovation, market-based incentives, and real public accountability. That's a winning approach to environmental progress, not only for this generation but for generations to come.

CHAPTER NINE

THE MORAL BASIS
OF A FREE SOCIETY

WHEN THE GOVERNMENT of China tells people they can read state-run newspapers, but not print and distribute Bibles (dissenters risk imprisonment and torture); or have one child, but not two (women are forced to have abortions); or watch state-run television, but not listen to Radio Free Asia (broadcast signals are jammed and students are threatened)—that is not freedom.

But the absence of centralized state control is not necessarily freedom either. The people of Beirut are not free. Neither are the people of Medellin and Cartagena, the drug capitals of Colombia. Freedom is not anarchy, chaos, and mayhem. The freedom to "let soulless forces operate," as the great economist Ludwig Von Mises termed it, is actually tyranny in another guise.

So what is freedom? How can a widely pluralistic society sustain freedom without degenerating into chaos? What is the moral basis of a free society? Today, the citizens and leaders of every nation are looking to America for answers to these questions. From Mexico City to Moscow, from Johannesburg to Jerusalem, from Bombay to Beijing, people have an eye on America as they struggle to make the exciting but difficult transition to free markets, free elections, free speech, and free worship.

131

While others are looking to us, however, Americans themselves are seeking answers to some painful and bitter questions. Can a free society survive the collapse of the two-parent family, when one-third of children are born into homes without fathers? Can a free society long endure a culture in which newborn babies have been thrown into trash dumpsters and young people have doubled their rate of heroin use in a single decade?

As the twentieth century comes to an end, the world is learning from America that the economic and political freedoms that come from capitalism and democracy are the most powerful and productive way to organize society. At the same time, we in America are discovering that capitalism and democracy alone are not enough to sustain a healthy, vibrant society. We are learning the hard way that a self-governing nation must consist of self-governing individuals. A

A self-governing nation must consist of self-governing individuals.

breakdown in the moral fabric of society has dire consequences. An explosion of violence, crime, drug use, sexual promiscuity, and out-of-wedlock births undermines the blessings of liberty and prosperity.

The stakes, therefore, are enormous. If America makes the economic, political, and moral changes necessary to move forward in the years ahead, then the rest of the world has a chance to get it right. But if America drifts off course, then the rest of the world will be in trouble as well.

WHAT IS FREEDOM?

Americans have always defined true freedom as an environment in which one may resist evil and do what is right, noble, and good without fear of reprisal. It is the presence of justice, tempered with mercy. It is a rule of law based on fundamental moral truths that are easily understood and fairly and effectively administered. It offers individuals and families equal opportunity to better their lives, morally, spiritually, intellectually, and economically.

Freedom, in other words, is neither a commodity for dictators to distribute and deny at will nor a moral, spiritual, or political vacuum in which anything goes. Freedom is a priceless treasure that the state is supposed to safeguard. Why? Because human beings have an intrinsic right to be free, a right that comes not from the state but from God. To the Founding Fathers, this was a "self-evident" truth. It is the essence of the American experiment in self-government.

The Founders, even those most suspicious of organized religion, believed that man's place in the universe was no accident—that man himself and the world in which he lived were created and sustained by a just and loving God. "It is impossible to account for the creation of the universe without the agency of a Supreme Being," wrote George Washington, and "it is impossible to govern the universe without the aid of a Supreme Being." James Madison put it this way: "The belief in a God All Powerful, wise and good, is so essential to the moral order of the World and to the happiness of man, that arguments which enforce it cannot be drawn from too many sources...."

To navigate the oceans without consulting fixed stars, Americans knew, is to risk being turned around by waves and wind, circling aimlessly with dwindling stores of food and water. To believe in the randomness of man's appearance on the earth, the Founders likewise intuitively understood, would be to deny the existence of fixed moral truths, established outside of man's own personal whims and predilections. In such a world, no one could judge with authority what is right or wrong because everyone would be entitled to his own value system. Hence, there could be no equality before the law, because the law would consist of whatever people in power declared it to be. That would elevate jungle law—what Darwin would later term as "survival of the fittest" over the rule of natural law. And that, in turn, would legitimize both the centralized European regimes of the Founders' day and the anarchic Beiruts of our day, where the powerful rule over the weak, use force to obtain riches, and use riches to reinforce their power.

Instead, the Founding Fathers staked the future of the country on the principle that human beings are created by God, and therefore have certain intrinsic, absolute, nonnegotiable rights. "All men are created equal," reads the Declaration of Independence, "and are endowed by their Creator with certain unalienable rights, that among these are life, liberty and the pursuit of happiness." Government's role in society, then, is to "secure these rights," not create or dispense them. This is the moral basis of a free society.

The order of these rights—first life, then freedom, and then the equal opportunity to pursue one's own happiness—was written with great care and precision, not haphazardly. The Founders understood the need to balance man's right to be free with man's responsibility to be honest, just, and fair. For example, if it makes you happy to shoot and kill someone while you rob a bank, the law says you're out of luck. A person's right to live supersedes your "freedom" to steal and murder. This may seem obvious, but it is profound. It is also the linchpin of Western civilization. Switch the order of these fundamental human rights—putting happiness before liberty, or liberty before life—and you end up with moral chaos and social anarchy. Deny the God-given nature of these rights, and you open the door to tyranny.

"Can the liberties of a nation be sure when we remove their only firm basis, a conviction in the minds of the people, that these liberties are the gift of God?" asked Thomas Jefferson. Or, as John Adams put it: "We have no government armed with power capable of contending with human passions unbridled by morality and religion. Avarice, ambition, revenge or gallantry would break the strongest cords of our Constitution as a whale goes through a net. Our Constitution was made only for a moral and religious people. It is wholly inadequate to the government of any other."

The people of the former Soviet Union are discovering this the hard way, in a tragic drama we have been tracking with great interest and concern at *Forbes* magazine. Communism destroyed not only material progress there but also the moral and spiritual foundations of the country. Trust between strangers, the fundamental moral component of a free market economy, barely exists. Without trust, how do you sign or enforce business contracts? How do you operate a system of credit? How do you maintain a basic sense of order? The people of the former Soviet Union are discovering that a free, self-governing society is nearly impossible without a moral foundation. Theft is rampant. Their murder rate is several times our own. Mafias are moving into the vacuum left by the fall of communism to seize control of vast sectors of economic activity. A Hobbesian world has emerged, where life is "nasty, brutish, and short."

> One of the great strengths of the American democracy is when we do stumble we have a history of rediscovering our first principles and resuming the journey toward faith and moral renewal.

AMERICA'S MORAL CRISIS

In America today, however, not everyone regards these basic moral truths as "self-evident." Modern liberalism, which rejects absolute moral standards, has abandoned the proper ordering of man's fundamental rights. As a result, modern liberalism has undermined a long-held American principle: that the law should protect the weakest of us, not just the strong, the healthy, and the rich. Abortion and euthanasia violate this principle by removing the protection of the law from society's most vulnerable members.

There is no need here to catalog in detail the lamentable results since the 1960s of liberalism's passions. The effort to legitimize all moral claims, to give personal freedom an utterly free hand—to "define deviancy down"—has given us horrific increases in violent crime, out-of-wedlock births, family breakups, and substance abuse; dramatic declines in educational and cultural standards; a proliferation of increasingly bizarre lawsuits; a blizzard of regulations that defy common sense and assault our rights to property and due process; a growing corruption of the tax code; and a judiciary that often acts like an imperial aristocracy hurling decrees down on the rest of us.

Modern liberalism has adopted a view of liberty that is at the same time too broad and too narrow. Liberalism wrongly insists, for example, on a parent's freedom to choose an abortion while simultaneously denying parents freedom to choose the schools that their children may attend.

Ideas have consequences. Liberalism's moral confusion over the sanctity of human life and the vital importance of the traditional family has reshaped American law and society. The statistics are grim enough. But the anecdotal evidence hits home: An eighteen-year-old girl attending her senior prom in New Jersey allegedly delivered her baby in a restroom, disposed of it in a plastic bag where it suffocated to death, cleaned herself up, and went back to the dance floor, where she asked the deejay to play a favorite song. A teenage couple in Delaware was charged with giving birth to a baby boy in a motel and then tossing him into a trash dumpster, where he died a cold, horrifying death. A fifteen-year-old boy in Detroit who "disappeared" for six months was found to have been sold by his mother to a drug dealer to cover a $1,000 cocaine debt. Meanwhile, "Doctor" Jack Kevorkian claims to have "assisted" in over one hundred "suicides" and now has been convicted of killing a man on prime-time television.

Certainly, crime is not new. But Americans have rarely been so confused about right and wrong, about what is acceptable and what is to be forcefully condemned.

So we must be clear: a free society cannot survive the collapse of the two-parent family or the absence of fathers, love, and discipline in the lives of so many children. A free society cannot survive an unchecked explosion in violent crime. Nor can a free society survive a generation of crack babies and teenagers whose minds and bodies have been destroyed by illegal drugs.

Like millions of people, my wife and I are deeply concerned about the moral condition of our nation. We are raising five daughters in a society whose wheels, it often seems, are coming off. It is difficult enough in any era to raise young girls to become wise and virtuous young women. But it is particularly difficult today. Movies, television, music, and the Internet bombard young people with messages of the sexual revolution and a materialistic, self-absorbed culture that tempt them away from good moral character rather than appealing to the better angels of their natures. Affluence does not protect children from temptation; sometimes it makes temptation more accessible.

The good news is that this is not the first time we have faced such dark times and turned things around. America has seen several periods of renewal and reform, such as the Great Awakening of the early eighteenth century—which set the social and spiritual stage for the Revolutionary War—and the Second Great Awakening of the early nineteenth century—which marked a return to America's founding ideals and helped an increasingly industrialized society strengthen its moral commitments while expanding personal freedom. Let us consider for a moment the latter of the two.

THE SECOND GREAT AWAKENING

Following the Revolutionary War, America experienced a period of moral decline. The chaos of battle, the pain of death and separation, the anxiety of war-time inflation, the excitement of subsequent political change, and the all-consuming nature of building a new nation drained people's time and energy. Fewer and fewer people attended church. Spiritual devotion waned, and social problems proliferated. From the late 1770s until the late 1820s, per capita consumption of alcohol in America rose dramatically, to about four to five times per person what it is today. Everybody took a swig from the jug—teachers, preachers, children. They called it "hard cider," but it was nothing like the cider we buy at the grocery store today. In those days, it seemed everyone was in a haze by noontime. The social consequences were predictable.

"Illegitimate births were rampant" during the early 1800s, wrote Tom Phillips, in his book *Revival Signs*. "Alcohol, the drug of the day, was destroying families and wrecking futures. Thomas Paine was proclaiming that Christianity was dead—and certainly the body of faith appeared to be in a coma. Yet even as Church rolls were shrinking and greed, sensuality, and family breakdown were becoming more widespread, America was about to experience a great spiritual revival."

Slowly at first, then building over the next several decades, one wave of spiritual renewal and religious rededication after another swept the country, in what historians now call America's "Second Great Awakening."

In one community after another, people began to wake up from their moral and spiritual slumber as though saying, "If we're going to have a self-governing nation, it must be occupied by self-governing citizens." The first public health movement in America was launched not by the government but by citizen activists such as Lyman Beecher, the founder of the American Bible Society and a pastor who went on to form the American Society for the Promotion of Temperance in 1826. This enterprise became known as the Temperance Movement—and it worked. Within one generation alcoholic consumption in America fell by two-thirds.

Soon pastors and community leaders were opening elementary and secondary schools (this was before "public" education), founding colleges and universities, setting up orphanages and homes for abandoned children, creating shelters for the poor, building hospitals, and exhorting people to stop drinking and spend more time with their families. The Reverend Thomas Gallaudet opened his school for the deaf. William McGuffey wrote his famous "Eclectic Readers," of which 120 million copies were printed. The first Young Men's Christian Association (YMCA) opened in Boston, followed shortly by the first Young Women's Christian Association.

It was during this rebuilding of the moral foundations of our free society that French historian Alexis de Tocqueville came to America in 1831. "Upon my arrival in the United States, the religious aspect of the country was the first thing that struck my attention, and the longer I stayed there, the more I perceived the great political consequences resulting from this new state of things," he wrote. "In France I had almost always seen the spirit of religion and the spirit of freedom marching in opposite directions. But in America I found they were intimately united and that they reigned in common over the same country."

Eventually, the religious and moral renewal of the Second Great Awakening gave birth to the abolitionist movement against slavery—one of the nation's greatest struggles to reassert a moral order of man's fundamental rights.

This gets to one of the great strengths of the American democracy. It is not that we do not make mistakes as a people and as a nation. We are, after all, only human. But when we do stumble and fall we have a history of rediscovering our first principles and resuming the journey toward faith and moral renewal.

RENEWAL AND THE
TWENTY-FIRST CENTURY

As we prepare to enter the twenty-first century, the American experiment is again being severely tested. The stakes are greater than they were in the early stages of the American experiment. It is not only our own future that is at stake, but ultimately the world's. Can we renew the moral and spiritual foundations of our free society?

I believe we can, in part because today we can once again see encouraging signs of moral and spiritual renewal in this country. Consider, for example, the tone of the welfare debate, which focused not on the fact that billions of dollars are being spent but on the fact that welfare is destroying the lives of the very people it was created to help. With less federal interference, many governors and mayors have been making dramatic reforms to help people move from welfare to work. They are urging churches, civic groups, and local businesses to help educate and employ welfare recipients—and Americans are rising to the challenge. Welfare rolls nationwide have dropped dramatically since 1996. In Wisconsin alone, welfare rolls have dropped by 84 percent over the past three years.

At the same time, millions of baby boomers are returning to churches and synagogues for the first time in years, some to meet their own spiritual needs and some to build strong moral foundations within their children. Willow Creek Community Church outside of Chicago, for example, attracts more than 15,000 people every weekend. Millions of high school students are also meeting for prayer and Bible study in small groups all over the country. James Dobson's *Focus on the Family* radio ministry is heard on more than 1,500 stations and is having remarkable success teaching couples to build strong, successful marriages and raise morally healthy children. As previously mentioned, William Bennett's *Book of Virtues*, an eight-hundred–plus page compilation of old poems, songs, and stories written to develop character, rocketed to the top of the best-seller list not long ago. His wife, Elayne, runs a successful sexual abstinence program for teenage girls in Washington, D.C. Meanwhile, Wade Horn's National Fatherhood Initiative and Charles Ballard's Institute for Responsible Fatherhood and Family Revitalization encourage

The Founders never intended the separation of church from state to become a separation of religion from public and civic life.

young men to take parenthood seriously. And these are just a few of many examples.

Consider, too, the Promise Keepers movement, an impressive series of rallies held in America's stadiums aimed at helping men make and keep seven promises ranging from racial reconciliation to being a good husband and father. Launched in 1990 by former University of Colorado football coach Bill McCartney, the first gathering drew 72 men. By 1994 a series of regional conferences were held drawing more than 280,000 men. By 1996 Promise Keepers' conferences had attracted more than 1,000,000 men from all over the country. In October of 1997 hundreds of thousands of men attended a single Promise Keepers event in Washington, D.C., not to call for political change, but to commit themselves to personal change.

Some Americans are uneasy with such public demonstrations of religious faith. But this is not new to American history either. "The first time I heard in the United States that a hundred thousand men had bound themselves together publicly to abstain from spirituous liquors," wrote Tocqueville, "it appeared to me more like a joke than a serious engagement." He added, "I did not at once perceive why these temperate citizens could not content themselves with drinking water by their own firesides." But Tocqueville was eager to learn. "I at last understood that these hundred thousand Americans, alarmed by the progress of drunkenness around them, had made up their minds to patronize temperance. They acted just in the same way as a man of high rank who should dress very plainly, in order to inspire the humbler orders with a contempt of luxury."

One of the most encouraging signs of moral and spiritual awakening occurred amidst the horror of the school shootings in Littleton, Colorado, in April of 1999. During the rampage that fateful spring day, one of the killers approached young Cassie Bernall, seventeen, shoved a gun in her face, and demanded to know, "Do you believe in God?"

"Yes," she replied.

The gunman reportedly laughed and said, "Why?" Then he pulled the trigger and killed her.

Rarely have Americans experienced such an act of unspeakable evil. Rarer still have we witnessed such an act of faith and courage, especially from a victim so young. In an age of such widespread spiritual emptiness among young people, Cassie Bernall had found real meaning and purpose. Friends say she had a quiet, simple faith, one that had dramatically transformed her life just two years earlier from one of loneliness, moodiness, and experimentation with the occult to one of deep personal conviction that God had a purpose and a plan for her.

News of her remarkable demonstration of heroism and martyrdom—and that of three other evangelical Christians and four Catholics—has inspired young people all over the country. At memorial services throughout Littleton, dozens of fellow classmates made professions of their newfound faith in God. Across the country, thousands of students—including 73,000 teens in Pontiac, Michigan, alone—gathered together to pray and rededicate their lives to God. In Wichita, Kansas, a twelve-year-old sixth-grade girl—inspired by Cassie Bernall's faith—told *Time* magazine: "If there was a shooter in my school, I'd volunteer to sacrifice my life. I'd say, 'Don't shoot my friends; shoot me,' because I know where I'll go when I die."

Referring to Cassie: "She was just like every other teenage kid," her youth pastor, Dave McPherson, told a reporter. "She wanted popularity, thought maybe she weighed a little too much, when she would dance, she wasn't in tune…. Cassie wasn't perfect. But you don't have to be perfect to be a martyr. You just have to be prepared, and Cassie was. She was prepared to give up her life."

In doing so, I believe Cassie Bernall may very well have set into motion a spiritual revival that could rescue a lost and hurting generation of young people.

WHAT IS GOVERNMENT'S ROLE?

Samuel Johnson once wrote, "How small, of all that human hearts endure/That part which laws or kings can cause or cure!" How true. Personal, moral, and spiritual renewal must happen in families, churches, and synagogues, as is beginning to happen. But government leaders do have a limited and specific role to play in reestablishing the moral foundation of a free society.

Presidents, senators and other government officials are not archbishops. They do not have primary responsibility for the life of the spirit. Yet our early presidents and other leading Founders knew well how crucial religion is to the cause of liberty. (To see this, you need only consult Article I of the early constitutions of the Commonwealths of Massachusetts, Pennsylvania, and Virginia). The great historian of liberty Lord Acton wrote that the history of liberty is in fact "coincident" with the history of Christianity, sprung from Judaism. In the words of Jefferson, "God who gave us life, gave us liberty." To save liberty, our Founders never failed to stress the role of faith.

At a particularly difficult impasse at the Constitutional convention in Philadelphia, Ben Franklin proposed a pause for solemn prayer to Providence, just as in *The Federalist Papers*, Madison, Hamilton, and Jay three times noted the interventions of divine Providence in the cause of establishing freedom on this continent. Presidents have declared national days of Thanksgiving to Almighty God. The inaugural speeches of Washington, Jefferson, and Lincoln—to take but three examples—are breathtaking for their moral and religious reach.

In short, our national leaders have often sensed a duty to express this nation's need of divine guidance and its gratitude for the Creator's manifold acts of assistance. In this country, we do not have an established church. But the foundations of our liberty are dug deep in the voluntary and heartfelt faith of millions.

To root our liberties more firmly in a moral soil, presidents and other officials can also show leadership in word, in deed, and in law.

Here are a few examples:

- Appoint judges and Supreme Court justices who respect the moral outlook that produced the Constitution they are interpreting. Such judges will not imagine themselves philosopher-kings who can dispense with centuries of ethical tradition or singlehandedly determine difficult social questions for an entire nation.

- Reinforce the concept that marriage is a legally binding contract. Most Americans still marry in places of worship, acknowledging the sacred nature of the vows they make to one another. To them, of course, marriage is much more than a legal contract, but it certainly is not less than one.

- Reform adoption laws to make it easier for loving, married couples to care for abandoned children. This would signal an awareness that all children have a fundamental right to loving parents, a right that supersedes claims by the state or of special-interest groups.

- Reject racial discrimination in all its guises, including quotas and set-asides. Equality in the eyes of the law is one of the most important ways we affirm the dignity and worth of all people.

- Protect people of all faiths—or of no faith—from encroachments by the state that violate their consciences and most deeply held beliefs. The Founders never intended the separation of church from state to become a separation of religion from public and civic life. There is no reason why a child should be denied the right to hold a Bible study before or after school, or write an essay about a biblical figure during school.

Each of these functions is rooted in the principle that government's role is to "secure" individual rights, not create new rights or dispense existing ones arbitrarily. Thus, the state must "establish justice, insure domestic tranquillity, provide for the common defence, promote the general welfare, and secure the blessings of liberty." No individual, family, or private institution can protect life, freedom, and property by apprehending criminals, trying them before a court of law, and incarcerating them. Nor can individuals and institutions, by themselves, enforce contracts, or fight terrorism, or negotiate and sign treaties with foreign governments, and the like. These are responsibilities to which only the state can attend. The Founders wrote the Constitution and the Bill of Rights to define precisely government's limited, specific role in securing individual rights, and how government should carry out that very important role.

Writing in defense of the Constitution, James Madison noted in *The Federalist* Number 51 that "if men were angels, no government would be necessary." But men are not angels. They are prone to attack, abuse, and impose upon the lives, liberties, and property of others. Therefore, Madison went on to assert, "justice is the end of government," its highest purpose and mission.

Conservatives have been accused of denying any significant role for government in promoting a just and healthy civil society. The accusation is utterly misguided. Government has a profoundly important role in recognizing and defending Americans' fundamental rights. Indeed, when the issue is the right to life—that is, defining the boundaries of the human community—government has no higher calling. And this is not just a matter for the states: the federal government has always had the responsibility, whether it acknowledged it or not, to secure this highest, most cherished of rights. That responsibility is again being severely debated and tested today.

Part of the reason for this social and political tension is that we as a nation seem so unclear about the proper ordering of our fundamental rights—the right to life, to liberty, and to the pursuit of happiness. As a result, there are at least three issues that serve as flashpoints for this debate: abortion, doctor-assisted suicide, and the battle against illegal drugs. Each is a life issue; each has become embroiled in arguments over the relationship between life and liberty.

ABORTION

Many Americans are uncomfortable discussing abortion, and understandably so; it is not a pleasant topic.

Today, however, there is no doubt—medically, genetically—that individual human life begins at conception and ends with natural death. The starting place for the discussion, then, is the recognition that abortion involves the violent ending of life—the first and foremost of our natural rights, the one that trumps all others. That is why abortions are a moral wrong and a national tragedy. As Lincoln said of slavery 140 years ago, abortion is and must be put on the road to extinction.

The real question is: How do we achieve this goal of making abortions disappear? We must recognize that we as a nation lack an overwhelming consensus about the primacy of life over liberty or the pursuit of happiness. We must recover such a consensus, but we cannot do so simply with the stroke of a legislative pen or a Supreme Court vote. In democracy, we cannot impose; we must persuade. Thus, the only way for abortions to disappear in this country is for there to be a change of heart, a change of conscience, a change of attitude. In order to change the law, we must change the culture. To change the culture, we must change the law step by step. I took a lot of heat for this view during the 1996 Republican presidential primaries, but as the political passions of the moment have settled, I think more people are recognizing that this approach makes eminent sense if we are to achieve our goal of protecting all human life.

We must all acknowledge that there has been a little legislative progress in restricting abortions since 1973, but only a little. Still, that is only part of the story. What is exciting is that change *outside* of Washington is truly visible. The number of abortions performed has declined to its lowest point since 1976. The number of doctors

willing to perform abortions has fallen. The number of schools willing to teach students about abortion is down dramatically.

Why is this? Because since 1973, when the practice of abortion
was legalized, the medical knowledge about birth available to doctors and the public has advanced by giant steps. We now have a
knowledge of the genetics of the first human cells, we have sonograms, and we have many more lifesaving techniques for infants
threatened in the womb.

In this changing moral climate, now is the time to advance the
issue legislatively, step by step. We should start by banning partial
birth abortions, a euphemism for infanticide. Support for a ban is
growing. We should also ban abortions for the purpose of sex selec-
tion, ban fetal tissue research, and end all federal funding for
abortion. As the father of five children, I also support parental noti-
fication and consent in the case of minors. We must also work to
end abortions in late pregnancy, unless the life of the mother is at
stake. Our hospitals today are like a house divided. In one room,
doctors work heroically to save a premature baby at twenty-two or
twenty-three weeks. Most of those babies now survive. Yet, in
another room, physicians and nurses work to kill a baby at that same
stage of the pregnancy. This house divided is untenable.

So where there is consensus on limiting abortions, let us codify.
From there, let us engage in a national conversation and seek to persuade those who disagree. I'm an optimist. I believe the country is
already moving in the right direction. Eventually, I believe we can
pass a human life amendment to protect all unborn children. Great
social change has happened before in American history, and I
believe that it can happen again.

DOCTOR-ASSISTED SUICIDE

At the other end of life, government must protect the elderly as well.
Our nation should not be misled. Assisted suicide will lead us down
the path to a dreary and dangerous society. At the altar of liberty, the

Jack Kevorkians of the world are prepared to sacrifice the inherent value of all human life.

My mother died from lung cancer seven years ago. Near the end the doctors asked her if she wanted a living will. She thought they meant that they wanted to pull the plug and she was outraged. She said, "No way—I'm fighting this to the end." My brothers and family and I were inspired by that. Just as we drew strength from her in adversity, she drew strength because we rallied around her in adversity. The medical profession must do more to alleviate physical pain. Its relative lack of progress here is a critical reason why assisted suicide, not to mention drug legalization, has made inroads with public opinion. While science makes progress on the physical side, we must work to provide real relief on the emotional and spiritual side, supporting others when they are in need.

Doctor-assisted suicide is the first step toward euthanasia, which is turning doctors the world over from healers into killers. Doctor-assisted suicide is not about people being on a respirator where technicians can barely find a brain wave. Nor is it about people who voluntarily refuse heroic measures. Rather, this is about what has happened in Holland, where they effectively legalized euthanasia. Since then, thousands of patients have been killed without their permission. With legalized assisted suicide, families will become greedy for their inheritance. The elderly will feel guilty for carrying on. People will say, "You're using up resources that others could use." Some day people may say that to you and me. It is a cold, grim road for society to take. It encourages the elderly to believe they are obstacles, not human beings reflecting God's image. We must fervently fight it every inch of the way.

DRUG LEGALIZATION

Finally, there is the issue of illegal drugs, which are destroying so many young people. This, too, is an issue where life supersedes liberty. Illegal drugs imprison drug takers within sometimes violent and murderous obsessions. Drugs are designed to alter our moral sensibilities, to dull our sense of duty and integrity. Addictive drugs are wrong because they enslave and eventually destroy the body. They take away free choice—the hallmark of human dignity. When the world of adults winks and nods at drug use, we aband on children to emotional and moral chaos, thus threatening their very lives.

We must not be misled by state initiatives that claim to legalize drugs only for medicinal purposes. Relieving pain and legalization are separate and distinct issues. America must not be made safe for Colombian-style drug cartels. Americans overwhelmingly reject the notion that someone's "freedom" to grow, sell, and use deadly drugs overrides society's right to protect lives. If an illegal drug contains a property that helps people in pain, that property should be extracted, or synthetically manufactured, and given to patients under proper medical supervision. The drug Marinol, for example, treats cancer and AIDS patients with a synthetic form of an active ingredient found in marijuana. But it is safe and available legally by prescription, without exposing users to more than four hundred other toxic chemicals found in smokeable "pot." By stepping up the efforts to combat and relieve pain, the medical profession will enormously enhance the quality of life for afflicted patients and remove the major motivator for drug legalization.

> **Great social change has happened before in American history, and I believe that it can happen again.**

Parents must repeatedly emphasize to their children how dangerous drugs can be. But society also has a right to protect itself from mind-altering, life-threatening drugs by the rule of law and its effective enforcement. Government must not use the fight against drug distribution and abuse as a license to deny individuals their constitutional rights. That said, however, the vast majority of Americans want a vigorous, effective fight against drugs. At the Democratic National Convention in 1992, Governor Bill Clinton told the nation that George Bush "hasn't fought a real war on crime and drugs. I will." But as president, he has not kept his commitment on one of the greatest causes of crime and human destruction.

THE UNFINISHED CHALLENGE

America's moral and creative energies have always come from the ground up. When Tocqueville visited America more than 160 years ago, he noticed the enormous energy that comes from people laboring together voluntarily—through churches and synagogues, schools, hospitals, sports, cultural activities, and professional activities—for a shared goal and purpose. That is the great, historic strength of America. Today, I believe that we are beginning another Great Awakening—and none too soon.

From the beginning of our nation's history, Americans have understood that freedom has three vital components: economic, political, and moral. In the twentieth century, the argument for economic freedom—that free markets and entrepreneurship are vital to social and economic progress—has largely been won. No one, outside of entrenched elites on some of our university faculties, argues that centralized control and ownership of a nation's economy will lead to freedom and prosperity. The battle now is to expand economic freedom while shrinking big government, both here in America and around the world.

The same is true with the argument for political freedom. In this century, we have witnessed and participated in brutal battles over the right of self-determination. People everywhere understand that they have an intrinsic right to free speech and free and fair elections. Here at home, people understand that government has gotten too big, promised too much, and delivered too little. More than that, where government has advanced, personal freedom and responsibility have retreated. Our challenge is to reform our corrupt political institutions here at home while setting an example for others struggling to determine their own destinies.

Yet the argument that there must be a moral basis undergirding a free society is one of the great unfinished challenges of our time. We have neglected the vital task of properly teaching our children, reminding ourselves, and communicating to others that man's rights to live free, pursue happiness, and own property come from God and are to be secured by the state. We have failed to assert at home and overseas the fundamental importance of spiritual faith and religious liberty in sustaining both freedom and democracy. Indeed, too often we have averted our eyes from those suffering persecution and even genocide.

As we end this bloody and brutal century, however, we must acknowledge that neglecting the moral basis of freedom has been terribly costly. We must also commit ourselves to a different road as we head into the twenty-first century.

America today is on the verge of the greatest era of economic freedom and spiritual renewal the world has ever seen. As we have done numerous times in our national history, we can once again brighten economic prospects for everyone, reform our corrupt political institutions, and restore the severely weakened moral foundations of our country. In so doing, we can truly fulfill our national destiny as the leader of a free world.

CHAPTER TEN

THE DEFENSE OF
A FREE SOCIETY

NEVER BEFORE IN human history has a nation occupied the position of strength and influence that America does today. The end of the Cold War and the fall of the Berlin Wall mean that we are the world's only superpower. The dawn of a new, high-tech, Information Age revolution means that we also have the world's most powerful economy. As a result, the world is looking to us to be an example of how a free people can adapt to—and move forward in—changing times and circumstances.

The opportunities before us are exhilarating. We can help people all around the world experience a new birth of freedom. We can help democratic capitalism sink real roots in once rocky and hostile soil, and by expanding free markets and free elections we can enhance our own security and expand our own prosperity. If America gets it right in the months and years ahead, the rest of the world has a chance to get it right. But if America gets in trouble, the rest of the world will be in trouble as well. It is just that simple.

The question before us, then, is this: Will we seize the tremendous opportunities that lie before us to ensure a new century of peace and prosperity? Or will we be condemned by future generations as an era of missed opportunities?

I happen to be an optimist. In part, this is because our history has long been shaped by men and women of remarkable vision, wisdom, and real personal courage who understood the times and knew what America should do. Why should we not believe that leaders of similar vision and character will once again emerge?

By expanding free markets and free elections we can enhance our own security and expand our own prosperity.

My optimism also stems from the fact that we have a unique opportunity to use America's high-tech advantage to stay ahead of our current and future adversaries. New technology can help provide more accurate intelligence on the military power and political intentions of other countries, particularly critical in light of China's disturbing military buildup. It can also help us develop better defenses. But nothing positive will happen unless we make the most of such opportunities, just as Ronald Reagan did to win the Cold War.

One of the most serious challenges we face, however, is that the Clinton-Gore administration seems to have set out to undo the Reagan legacy. It is systematically dismantling America's military capabilities and destroying America's credibility around the world. Indeed, this administration has acted as a universal solvent, corroding the pillars of strength upon which our economic and national security rest. This is a potential time bomb waiting to go off. We must defuse it and once again focus on the defense of our free society.

- *We must stop playing politics with foreign policy and start putting America's vital national security interests first.*
- *We must stop cutting back on national defense and start restoring the strength of America's military.*
- *We must restore honesty and integrity to America's foreign policy.*

As the chief executive of an American company who has traveled to and done business in more than sixty countries around the world, I have long had a deep interest in foreign policy and national security issues. In fact, from the time my grandfather left Scotland to come to America, our family has taken a keen interest in the defense and expansion of freedom.

My father was a machine gunner in the American army during World War II. Seriously wounded by enemy gunfire, he spent a great deal of time recovering in military hospitals. When he came back home he made sure that each of the five children he and my mother would have would come to understand the immense value and high price of liberty and the true virtue of American leadership. I was the first, born in 1947—an authentic baby boomer—and my father's love for his country and understanding of history and the world made a great impression on me. I would go on to gain a love for history in college and to serve in the National Guard as part of a field artillery unit. It was not heroic like my father's service, but it was honorable and it helped me gain a deeper appreciation for the military life and for the freedoms we can so easily take for granted.

If America gets it right in the months and years ahead, the rest of the world has a chance to get it right. But if America gets in trouble, the rest of the world will be in trouble as well.

Besides my own parents and grandparents, it was Ronald Reagan who taught me the most about the magic and mystery of freedom and America's responsibility to protect it. As a teenager in 1964, I remember sitting with my mother and father and some CEOs and their wives watching "Citizen Reagan" deliver his nationally televised speech, "A Time for Choosing," in support of Barry Goldwater. Despite the fact that Reagan was not an elected official—or perhaps because of it—his eloquent defense of American ideals and his challenge to Americans to choose not between right or left but between forward progress and cultural decline made a powerful impression on me.

BROADCASTING FREEDOM

Almost two decades later, in 1985, President Reagan would ask me to be chairman of the bipartisan Board for International Broadcasting, which oversees Radio Free Europe and Radio Liberty (RFE/RL), in what turned out to be the final years of the Evil Empire. For a second-generation American whose family business was all about communicating the message of free markets and free elections, it was an offer I could not refuse.

When I took the post I already knew that RFE/RL was a critical source of news, information, analysis, and debate for the people of Eastern and Central Europe and the Soviet Union. But I am not sure that at the beginning I fully appreciated the power of radio technology to bring hope to those living in fear and to inspire the imagination of people yearning to be free. It was something that I would come to learn from Ronald Reagan. Once a radio broadcaster himself, Reagan intuitively understood that radio broadcasting is one of the best ways to connect with the human heart. He believed passionately that it could be used to help create an environment for promoting truth, tolerance, pluralism, and democracy, and he wanted us to take full advantage of the technology to help spark a freedom revolution behind the Iron Curtain and then help democracy really take hold there.

That is precisely what we did. Radio Free Europe's Polish service, for example, provided a model of serious, Western-style coverage of candidates and issues during Poland's pivotal presidential election campaign in 1990. Our open coverage was in sharp contrast with an often biased, partisan, and sensational treatment by Polish state broadcast media. Lech Walesa was later asked what role Radio Free Europe played in events in Poland. "What is the earth without the sun?" he replied.

When Soviet security forces attacked Lithuanian broadcast facilities, killing fourteen civilians and provoking worldwide condemnation, Lithuania's democratically elected government barricaded itself in the parliament building and quickly established an open telephone line to RFE/RL in Munich. Over a critical twelve-hour period this line served as a principal channel of communications between the country's legitimate authorities and the outside world.

We also sought to keep alive indigenous cultures and make listeners aware of their country's pro-freedom artists. During the dark years of totalitarian repression, for example, we were the only international broadcaster to read in its entirety Solzhenitsyn's *The Gulag Archipelago*. We were also one of the few who repeatedly read Vaclav Havel's novels and plays and made him a household name in Czechoslovakia, even though he was being hounded by the communist regime.

I served as chairman of the Board for International Broadcasting from 1985 to 1993, and in those years had the opportunity to make a small but important difference in the lives of millions of people. I saw the scathing criticism President Reagan received for his tough, principled strategy to win the Cold War. I also saw his critics silenced (briefly, at least) by the fall of the Berlin Wall and the collapse of the Soviet empire. But what I will always remember most is the opportunity to witness firsthand the rebirth of freedom in Central and Eastern Europe and the Soviet republics. Much of the American political establishment said that it could not be done. But they could not have been more wrong.

Through my work with RFE/RL, I also had the opportunity to work with some remarkable men and women on the front lines of freedom—President Reagan's first defense secretary, Caspar Weinberger; Poland's Lech Walesa; Czechoslovakia's Vaclav Havel; Germany's Helmut Kohl; Canada's Brian Mulroney; and, of course, the indomitable British prime minister, Margaret Thatcher. Together with President Reagan, these are the heroes of the great freedom revolution of the 1980s. Today they are too quickly being forgotten by a world moving at light speed. But it was this core group of leaders, the caliber of which the world may not see again for some time, who truly understood the importance of peace through strength and of shining the light of truth on those hud-dled in the pitch-black darkness of communist tyranny.

When I took the helm at *Forbes* in 1990, I made it one of my top priorities to keep American business leaders on the cutting edge of national security developments and international economic issues. Cap Weinberger joined the magazine as publisher in 1988 and writes a column on foreign policy and national security affairs. He became chairman of Forbes, Inc., in 1993. We recently brought in Brian Mulroney as chairman of *Forbes Global Business & Finance*, the international publication we launched in 1998.

Today I am deeply concerned that we have a president who has squandered much of the moral and strategic capital that President Reagan built up during the 1980s. A great opportunity exists for a new century of free markets and free elections all around the world. But thanks to the Clinton-Gore administration's drift and indeci-sion, storm clouds are gathering on the horizon.

So what are the major challenges we face as we head into the twenty-first century, and how should we deal with them?

REBUILDING OUR INCREASINGLY HOLLOW MILITARY

Today, the United States spends less on defense as a percentage of our economy than we did at any time since the Japanese attack on Pearl Harbor. For the world's only superpower, that is an invitation to very serious trouble. As a naval power historically and geograph-ically, we have long relied on our ability to project military force wherever it is necessary. But our annual procurement of ships has dropped dramatically since the 1980s. The result? The 569-ship navy we had under President Reagan has been slashed to just 347 ships—a 40 percent reduction. The administration may also cut back further to just 310 ships by 2003.

The greatest symbol of American power projection is the air-craft carrier. For personnel and logistical reasons, carriers cannot be at sea constantly. Yet the administration has slashed the number of American carrier battle groups from fifteen to eleven. The effect? The U.S. can no longer have a carrier constantly stationed in all three sectors considered most strategically sensitive—the Indian Ocean and Persian Gulf region, the Mediterranean, and the Western Pacific. In our standoff with Saddam Hussein during the winter of 1997–98, did anyone notice that at the height of the crisis one of our three aircraft carriers deployed in the region had to depart the Gulf and return home? What a signal that must have sent Saddam. When China lobbed missiles off Taiwan in 1996 during the first fully democratic presidential election in over four thousand years of recorded Chinese history, the United States had to deploy two carriers to the Taiwan Strait. Will we have the naval power to do that again?

Today, the United States spends less on defense as a percentage of our economy than we did at any time since the Japanese attack on Pearl Harbor. For the world's only superpower, that is an invitation to very serious trouble.

The administration has also whacked the United States Marine Corps. The 199,000 active-duty marines have been reduced to 174,000. The corps's 42,000 reservists have been reduced to 37,000.

The administration has slashed the army by more than 40 percent. The army's active divisions have been reduced from eighteen to ten, while its reserve divisions have been reduced from ten to the equivalent of about five.

The administration has slashed the air force by nearly 50 percent. Where there were once twenty-six active tactical wings, now there are only thirteen. Where there were once thirteen reserve wings, now there are only seven. The air force also reports a serious shortage of pilots, a shortage that is expected to worsen over the next few years. The planes these pilots are flying are rapidly aging. Some, such as our B-52 bombers, are older than the pilots that are in them. Aircraft spare parts are getting so hard to come by that readiness experts talk these days of "cannibalization"—mechanics stripping parts from one plane to replace broken parts on other planes. And this isn't happening only on airplanes. It is happening throughout the Air Force on all kinds of weapons systems.

At the same time, the administration keeps stretching U.S. forces thinner and thinner, getting involved in regional conflicts with little or no strategic planning or sense of purpose. All of these problems—plus the lack of competitive pay—is starting to have a serious effect on morale in our armed forces, just as it did during the late 1970s.

Can we turn things around? Of course. But it is going to take real leadership that will seriously assess our situation and persuade the American people that business as usual will not be enough to protect us from threats that lie just over the horizon.

DEPLOYING STATE-OF-THE-ART BALLISTIC MISSILE DEFENSE SYSTEMS

How can Americans enjoy peace if they cannot be protected from ballistic missile attacks? The first challenge of leadership is to defend the homeland, and to do that we must rapidly deploy state-of-the art missile defense systems to protect Americans, as well as our allies.

During World War II, Nazi German missiles rained down terror on the people of Great Britain. Between 1944 and 1945, nearly 2 million British homes were damaged or destroyed and 67,000 casualties resulted. The missile raids "imposed on the people of London a burden heavier than the air raids of 1940 and 1941," Winston Churchill would later write. "The blind, impersonal nature of the missile made the individual on the ground feel helpless."

During the Gulf War, Americans watched on television with horror as Iraqi Scud missiles rained down on American forces in Saudi Arabia and on the people of Israel. We cheered as our Patriot missiles intercepted the Scuds, only to learn later that the Patriots had not performed nearly as effectively as we had thought at the time. Today, the threat of missile attack has grown much worse, but Washington still has not deployed a truly effective defense system.

The Central Intelligence Agency estimates that more than twenty countries are developing ballistic missiles. A chilling July 1998 report by former Defense Secretary Donald Rumsfeld found that a power of far less military might than the United States—such as Iran or North Korea—could wreak havoc on us by launching nuclear, chemical, or biological weapons via ballistic missiles, and that they could be ready to do so in the next five years. Consider just one excerpt from the unclassified report by the bipartisan Commission to Assess the Ballistic Missile Threat to the United States:

> There is evidence that North Korea is working hard on the Taepo Dong 2 (TD-2) ballistic missile.... This missile could reach major cities and military bases in Alaska and the smaller, western-most islands in the Hawaiian chain. Light-weight variations of the TD-2 could fly as far as 10,000 km, placing at risk western U.S. territory in an arc extending northwest from Phoenix, Arizona, to Madison, Wisconsin.

Most Americans do not even realize that the military they regard so highly lacks the capability to prevent devastation from missile attack. Yet to underscore how serious this threat really is, less than one week after the release of the Rumsfeld Commission's report, Iran tested the *Shahab-3*, a ballistic missile capable of hitting Israel. The following month North Korea tested a medium-range missile over the mainland of Japan. In December of 1998 Russia tested a new intercontinental ballistic missile. India and Pakistan have also tested nuclear weapons and the means to deliver them.

We could construct viable missile defense systems for ourselves and our allies in Europe, Israel, Japan, Taiwan, and South Korea—to name a few—by integrating new missile defense innovations with existing technologies on the Navy's Aegis cruisers. American tax-payers have already invested some $50 billion in missile defense research. Experts believe it would take less than $10 billion to finish the job. But the president and vice president continue to drag their feet. What in God's name are they waiting for?

The current administration also clings to the Anti-Ballistic Missile Treaty (ABM Treaty), which prevents the United States from fully developing effective missile defenses. The treaty was a bad idea during the Cold War, given its reliance on what defense expert Frank Gaffney calls "assured vulnerability." But it certainly makes no sense today. The nation that we signed the treaty with—the Soviet Union—no longer exists. So why are we abiding by the treaty's terms? The proliferation of weapons of mass destruction and the missiles to carry them makes the ABM Treaty an even worse idea—and missile defense an even better idea—today than when Ronald Reagan delivered his heroic speech announcing a "Strategic Defense Initiative" in 1983.

Here again, I am an optimist. New technologies—from advanced guidance systems to sophisticated satellite command and control systems—are making missile interceptors more feasible than ever before. What has been missing, thus far, is the political leadership to make it happen. But we can change that. That is one of the reasons the next election is so important. We could end all this foot-dragging and move with Manhattan Project–like speed to deploy state-of-the-art missile defense systems. The political establishment may not get it, but I believe that the American people will.

A U.S.—NOT A U.N.—FOREIGN POLICY

Another very serious challenge we face is the fact that the current administration does not seem to have a sense of strategic direction in this post–Cold War era. Just look at the crisis in the Balkans. Our government went in with grossly inadequate planning and preparation, thereby looking lost and indecisive.

We need a U.S.—not a U.N.—foreign policy. We cannot—and should not—pass the buck, so to speak, to others when formulating our approach. We have genuine strategic interests in Europe, much of Asia and the Pacific Rim, and, obviously, Latin America. Why, then, did the White House commit troops to remake Somalia and permit them to be humiliated by well-armed gangs? It is time for leaders who understand the times and know what America should do.

RUSSIA

Consider Russia, for example. Moscow still controls about twenty thousand nuclear weapons. Yet U.S.–Russian relations have been badly handled during the 1990s.

In a "Fact and Comment" column I wrote in *Forbes* in January of 1994, I warned of the dangers of neglecting the Russian economy: "To date, [President] Clinton has done less for Russia's economy than Calvin Coolidge did for Germany's in the mid-1920s. If the President doesn't want to be tagged with responsibility for 'losing' Russia to political extremists, he had better read up on how other countries have reestablished stable money."

Instead, the president and vice president have offered the Russians harmful, counterproductive economic advice. During the summer of 1998, for example, the vice president goaded the Kremlin to slap more taxes on an already teetering economy, including a new national sales tax, even though Russians are already suffering from an abominable tax "system" where there are more taxes than national income. This administration has also urged the Kremlin to listen closely to officials from the International Monetary Fund (IMF), who in turn urged Moscow to "improve" tax collections and to adopt other pieces of economically destructive advice. Not surprisingly, Kremlin officials have pocketed billions of dollars in "economic aid."

At the same time, the White House has never consistently, forcefully pushed for the establishment of the rule of law in Russia.

Instead, it has cynically turned a blind eye to wholesale thievery by well-connected figures in a system more accurately described as a kleptocracy than a democracy. Much of the money that the United States and the IMF provided Russia during the 1990s, for example, has been wasted. Large chunks were quickly diverted into the foreign bank accounts of Kremlin insiders. Even recently retired U.S. Treasury Secretary Robert Rubin has admitted this is so.

Moreover, the administration has not even launched the kind of exchange programs with Russia that were so successful in exposing thousands of up-and-coming Germans to the American way of life after World War II. As a result, the concept of democracy and free enterprise are being undermined in the minds of most Russians. They see them as a euphemism for organized robbery of the many by the few.

The results have not been pretty. Not since the early days of Weimar Germany after World War I—where similar failures fanned extremists, including the Nazis—has there been such a disaster in such an important country. A sixteen-year-old Russian male is now less likely to live to age sixty than one hundred years ago. The Russian economy is in serious trouble. Inflation has been rampant. People are suffering a lack of food outside the major cities. Communists and other anti-Western factions have been steadily gaining political strength. Boris Yeltsin's days in government are numbered. The aging leader is physically sick and politically weak. Who knows where a new regime could lurch?

So what should the United States be doing to help Russia move in the right direction? Our top priority must be to make it clear to all parties in the Russian government—and to the Russian people—that we want a peaceful and productive relationship with them, regardless of who is in power. One of the ways we can do this is to help the Russians stabilize their economy and get on the road to a healthy, growing, free-market system. More IMF loans are not the answer. Instead, we must advise Russia to follow the five essential principles of economic prosperity.

The first principle is to create a sound currency. This is not an option. It is a necessity. Without a stable ruble, no free-market reforms will succeed. Germany and Japan found themselves with virtually worthless currencies after World War II. But their eventual miraculous economic recoveries were all preceded by currency reforms. The same is true with countries like Argentina, which stabilized its currency, ended hyperinflation, and rescued its economy under the guidance of then–economic minister Domingo Cavallo, who subsequently served as publisher of *Forbes Global Business & Finance*. Yet the IMF—the Typhoid Mary of modern economies—typically encourages currency devaluations which lead to rampant inflation and severe economic distress for poor and middle-class working families.

The second principle is low taxes and tariffs. Germany and Japan reduced their tax rates in the late 1940s and early 1950s, and Korea did so in the 1960s. All saw their economic growth rise dramatically. Over the past several decades Hong Kong has also been an outstanding example of what such pro-growth incentives can do to create new wealth and a booming economy. High taxes and high tariffs do not create wealth—they destroy it. But, when President Reagan slashed taxes by 25 percent across the board, he helped lead the United States out of a severe economic recession and provided a model for others to follow.

The third principle is the rule of law, particularly individual equality before the law and property rights. The right to buy, hold, and sell property lies at the heart of all economic activity. Without such protections, why will people take risks and create new businesses if their assets can be seized by the government or stolen by others? How can entrepreneurs challenge powerful companies and interests without the protection of the law?

The fourth principle is minimal bureaucratic interference in the creation and expansion of small businesses. Too many rules, regulations, and bureaucratic labyrinths make it difficult if not impossible for would-be entrepreneurs to succeed. Yet small businesses are often the engine driving a country's economic growth and creating the vast majority of a country's new jobs. Why not make it easier for them to operate freely?

The fifth principle is that trade and business barriers must be removed. Make it easier for people to do business, and more business will be done.

It is essential that we help Russia put such principles to work. A stabilized Russian economy may be our best hope for helping support and strengthen pro-Western forces in the former Soviet Union and promoting a safer and freer world. At the same time, we should: dramatically step up the broadcasting of business news, free market educational programming, and interviews with successful entrepreneurs and small-business owners on Radio Liberty and Voice of America; bring Russian students over to study business, free markets, and free elections at U.S. universities; and help the Russian police learn to root out corruption and mob activity. We also need to do more to help the Russian military destroy its stockpile of weapons of mass destruction.

The big question is: Which route will Russia go—that of the weak and troubled Weimar Germany, or of the democratically robust Federal Republic of Germany that emerged from the ashes of World War II?

CHINA

The rise of China as a new power is another great challenge for the United States as we go into the twenty-first century. Our failure to properly handle the rise of Germany and Japan earlier in the twentieth century cost us and the world dearly. We must not make the same mistake with China.

Our president calls his China policy "constructive engagement." But it is better described as abject appeasement and a sellout of vital U.S. interests. If we continue the administration's drift and zigzagging, our children and grandchildren will ultimately pay the price.

We must be open and firm. But China doesn't know what the real rules of engagement are. After all, this president has quickly made threats and just as quickly backed down. Clearly, Beijing takes our president's statements no more seriously than he does.

Our ultimate hope for a fruitful, non-warlike relationship with the Middle Kingdom lies in the rise of pro-freedom, pro–free enterprise forces within it. Economic expansion and trade are essential for the growth of middle and entrepreneurial classes interested in peacefully improving their lot in life. As we have seen in Chile, South Korea, and Taiwan, economic liberalization can bring in its wake demands for political reform. Such a course is not inevitable— nothing in human affairs is—but it is our best hope.

Low tariff trade, however, should not mean "business as usual." The United States must clearly and consistently articulate and advance American strategic objectives in Asia:

1. We must make our military commitment to the region crystal clear, and we must remain strong, particularly in light of the growing Chinese military might.
2. We must promote fundamental human rights, including the rule of law, free markets, free elections, freedom of worship, freedom of the press, and freedom to own property.
3. We must open new markets and expand existing markets for U.S. goods and services.

To these ends, we should make it clear that we will defend Taiwan from attack. To give credibility to our military presence, the United States should expand military cooperation with allies in the region, rapidly deploy regional ballistic missile defenses, and pass a U.S. defense budget that truly pays for the necessary manpower and technology.

We should stop selling China sophisticated technology that it can use for military purposes. If Beijing sells prohibited military equipment to rogue states, we should apply sanctions. China was caught providing Pakistan with nuclear parts, and the administration did nothing. The Chinese army controls some fifteen thousand companies that have about $10 billion in worldwide sales. We should apply sanctions on some of the PLA companies doing business in the United States. If the offenses continue, we could slap penalties on more of these companies. China badly wants to join the World Trade Organization on concessionary terms. We should oppose this until we get to the bottom of the security-spying scandals. Then we must see if China is willing to meaningfully reduce trade barriers, especially as China poses an increasingly serious threat to U.S. and Asian security. We should also stop the World Bank from providing Beijing with subsidized loans.

At the same time, we should take the lead in forcefully and consistently denouncing China's human rights abuses. These abuses include suppressing Buddhists in Tibet and Christians in China; suppressing political dissidents; executing some prisoners to obtain their organs for sale, while exploiting others through slave labor to make products for export; carrying out forced abortions; and maintaining death-factory orphanages. Beijing will protest angrily. But pressure will yield results. We should also increase funding for the National Endowment for Democracy, and Radio Free Asia should have more programming and more power to send its signals so people can actually hear the broadcasts. Remember, radio offers a tremendous opportunity to communicate with the Chinese people about business, culture, faith, and international events. It can also offer interviews with Chinese dissidents about human rights abuses and the progress of the pro-democracy movement inside and outside of China. As I learned from my years with the Board for International Broadcasting, the free flow of truth is deadly to dictatorial regimes.

We must also move decisively to stop Chinese intelligence operations against the United States—particularly against U.S. nuclear laboratories. The bipartisan Cox Report—named after California Congressman Christopher Cox and released in May of 1999—

provided a chilling look into the magnitude of Chinese espionage and harmful U.S. technology transfers to the Chinese. Now we must dramatically step up our research and development to reopen the technology gap and pull away from our adversaries and potential adversaries. We must also learn the full truth about the serious and credible allegations that the Chinese government illegally funneled money into the American political system during the 1996 campaign.

Our approach toward China must not be "either/or"—either abject appeasement or total isolation. There are many tools in our diplomatic, economic, and national security toolbox. We must learn to use each of them wisely. But we must also be clear: if China desires confrontation, then Normal Trade Relations (formerly known as Most Favored Nation trading status) will end and America will vigorously defend her interests and her allies.

The White House's "see no evil, hear no evil, speak no evil" policy toward China is galling and symptomatic of a U.S.–China policy gone adrift. It is essential that the United States carry out a firm, coherent China policy—one of containment, of concern for human rights, of open trade, and of real determination. Clearly, the stakes are great, but so are the opportunities.

IRAQ

Nearly a decade after Operation Desert Storm, Saddam Hussein remains in power. He continues to develop weapons of mass destruction. He may also be experimenting on human prisoners with deadly biological toxins. Given the opportunity, he will undoubtedly use such weapons to intimidate his neighbors, particularly Kuwait and Saudi Arabia. If his ambitions are blocked, he could very well lob anthrax-laden missiles on Tel Aviv. He has also threatened a million-man "holy war" against the United States. If U.N. sanctions are lifted, Saddam will once again be able to sell oil and invest huge sums of new revenue to recreate his war machine.

The United States has consistently underestimated and misread this cunning mass murderer. Two decades ago, the State Department's spin was that Saddam was a moderate. Months later Iraq invaded Iran, setting off eight years of World War I–style bloodletting. No sooner did that conflict end than we put on our myopic glasses again. Our reward? Saddam grabbed Kuwait.

It is time, therefore, to make the fall of Saddam Hussein from power a top priority of U.S. policy in the Middle East. There will be no long-term peace and security in the region until he is gone.

We should start by supporting, training, and arming a counter-regime to Saddam Hussein to help Iraqis liberate Iraq from his evil vise-grip. We should release some of the frozen Iraqi financial assets to help fund this pro-freedom opposition. We should maximize the use of Radio Free Iraq to communicate news and vital information to the suffering Iraqi people and encourage the fledgling and embattled pro-democracy movement inside the country. We should expand the so-called "safe haven" in northern Iraq—and create a similar zone in the South—to protect Iraqi opposition forces and their families, and we should exclude Iraqi ground forces from entering these safe havens. At the same time, we should declare a no-fly zone over all of Iraq, not just the northern portion of it. After the 1991 Gulf War, anti-Saddam rebellions broke out in all parts of Iraq. Inexplicably—and inexcusably—Saddam was allowed to use his existing aircraft to rapidly crush these uprisings. A no-fly rule would dramatically tell potential rebels that Saddam would no longer be able to quickly put them down, and would encourage within the military what Saddam most fears, a real revolution.

Some say it would be impossible to end the reign of Saddam Hussein. Some say it is not even worth trying. But the same was said about Ronald Reagan's strategy to relegate the Evil Empire to the "ash heap of history." Sometimes the naysayers are wrong.

IRAN

Iran is one of our most serious challenges. Despite a "moderate" tone of late, many Iranian leaders hold deep-rooted and long-held hatred for the United States, the "Great Satan" of Western corruption and decadence. They despise the Iraqis for engaging them in a bloody, eight-year-long war in the 1980s. They despise the Saudis for bankrolling Iraq's war against them and for controlling the Islamic holy sites of Mecca and Medina. They also harbor a bloodlust against Israel.

Yet unlike Saddam Hussein—who invaded Kuwait before he had completed building his weapons of mass destruction—Iranian leaders are not likely to pursue their objectives or strike at their enemies before they have adequately prepared.

From Russia the Iranians have bought submarines to control the waters of the Persian Gulf and the Straights of Hormuz. From Russia, China, and North Korea, the Iranians have purchased ballistic missile technology to reach deep into the territory of their enemies. In camps scattered throughout the Middle East, the Iranians have developed terrorist hit squads capable of infiltrating their enemies and delivering death by stealth. In 1996, for example, nineteen American servicemen were killed and more than five hundred were wounded in the Khobar Towers bombing in Saudi Arabia. In 1997 U.S. and Saudi intelligence officials were able to link that bombing to a senior Iranian intelligence official. "Iran was the organizing force behind it," one U.S. official told the *Washington Post*.

But submarines, missiles, and terrorists are just delivery vehicles. The real concern to the West should be what is inside those vehicles, and this is where it becomes clear that Iran is emerging as one of the most serious threats to U.S. national security: Iran is building the Islamic Bomb—an arsenal of nuclear, chemical, and biological weapons capable of carrying out a genocidal "jihad."

From Russian and European sources Iran has been buying nuclear power plant technology, claiming it is all for peaceful purposes. But since Iran has some of the world's greatest oil and natural gas reserves and thus no need for nuclear power, Western experts have no doubt Iran is developing nuclear weapons. Iran also has a very active chemical warfare program. Now there is increasing evidence that Iran is intent on developing the most deadly biological weapons known to man.

"Iran is scouring the former Soviet Union to hire scientists who once worked in laboratories tied to Moscow's vast germ warfare program and has succeeded in recruiting some of them to take jobs in Teheran," wrote Judith Miller and William J. Broad in a December 1998 *New York Times* report called "The Germ Warriors." The article quoted a Russian biochemist who met with a delegation of Iranians and said "one thing they repeatedly asked about was human genetic engineering." As Miller and Broad reported: "[I]n germ weaponry, the possibility of attacking human genes is the most chilling of all, military experts agree. In theory, genetic engineering could produce weapons that kill or cripple selectively by race and nationality."

So what should the United States do to deal with the emerging threat from Iran? First and foremost we must deploy state-of-the-art ballistic missile defense systems. We must also beef up our intelligence-gathering efforts to get ahead of the curve on what Iran has and what it is planning. We must use all of our leverage to stop the flow of nuclear, chemical, biological, and ballistic missile technology into Iran, particularly from Russia, China, Europe, and Pakistan. We should strengthen our alliances with Israel, Saudi Arabia, Turkey, and the Persian Gulf States. We should also move quickly and decisively to use our advantage in sophisticated, twenty-first–century medical research and technology to prepare effective defenses against biological terrorism. That includes stockpiling existing vaccines and developing new vaccines and cures for a wide variety of threats, including viruses like anthrax, smallpox, and ebola. The nerve gas bombing in the Tokyo subway in March of 1995—which killed twelve people and injured five thousand more—should have been a wake-up call for the West. But to date, not nearly enough has been done to protect Americans at home and abroad.

We should also make full use of the Farsi-language radio broadcasting service (essentially a "Radio Free Iran" network, though it is not officially called that) begun in Prague, Czech Republic, in the fall of 1998 under the auspices of RFE/RL. As in other parts of the world, we should be providing news, analysis, opinion, and debate to a country that largely prohibits the free exchange of ideas. Indeed, we should be doing everything we can to help bolster pro-democracy, pro-freedom forces inside and outside of Iran and to expose Iranian human rights abuses and terrorist activity to the light of day.

CYBER-WARFARE

Another emerging threat to U.S. national security has received little attention but could loom large as we head into the twenty-first century: the rise of cyber-warfare. Even if the United States and the rest of the world make it through the Year 2000 computer crisis relatively unscathed, the world's computer systems are highly vulnerable to a new kind of high-tech combat that uses computer viruses to infect and destroy a nation's information technology systems. Military command-and-control systems are vulnerable, as are civilian communication systems, power grids, and banking and financial networks.

In March of 1999, retired Air Force General Robert T. Marsh told a Senate Armed Services subcommittee that the United States is not threatened only by weapons of mass destruction, but also by "weapons of mass disruption." He described a dangerous new world of computer " 'Trojan horses,' 'traps doors,' 'bombs,' and 'spamming' that can alter data, steal or destroy data, or deny service." Such weapons "can be used anywhere, anytime, by anyone with the capability and intent to do harm. They offer the advantage of anonymity, and when these tools are used, their effects can be magnified by the growing complexity and interdependence of our infrastructures. Such interdependence creates an increased possibility that a rather minor disturbance can cascade into a regional outage."

In 1997 the Pentagon conducted an exercise code-named "Eligible Receiver." It used teams of computer "hackers"—drawn from the ranks of the National Security Agency—to try to break in and shut down the Defense Department's most sensitive computer networks. The goal was to test the military's ability to withstand a sustained cyber-attack against its information technology systems. After only a few days into the two-week exercise it became painfully obvious that tremendous damage could be done in a very short time. Deputy Defense Secretary John Hamre testified to Congress in March of 1999 that "Eligible Receiver" demonstrated that the military had "little capability to detect or assess cyber attacks and that our 'indications and warning' process for cyber events was totally inadequate." The military has tried to correct this problem. But, Hamre said, "as we've improved our ability to monitor [computer] network activities, the number of probes, intrusions, and cyber events we can observe continues to increase. We are now detecting eighty to one-hundred events daily. Of these, approximately ten will require detailed investigation."

Businesses are also vulnerable to cyber-warfare. Just days after General Marsh testified to Congress about "weapons of mass disruption," the fastest-spreading computer virus in history—a virus known as "Melissa"—infected more than 100,000 computers around the world and shut down the information technology networks at hundreds of American companies. A New Jersey man was quickly arrested and charged. But the event was a jolt. Steve White, a senior anti-virus researcher at IBM, told the *New York Times*: "It's possible that in the near future, viruses could spread around the globe in a matter of an hour or two, and if it's a destructive virus, do incredible amounts of damage. It's going to demand an entire new way of combating them, new approaches and new technologies."

All of this underscores the importance of staying focused like a laser on solving the Year 2000 computer crisis at home and around the world, and taking the emerging threat of cyber-warfare very seriously. That means developing new strategies and new technologies to protect our economies from random and systematic attacks against our information infrastructures. In an Industrial Age economy, a disruption in the flow of oil—such as the Arab oil embargo in the early 1970s—can lead to severe global recessions, notes Edward Yardeni, an expert on the global economy. Yardeni also notes that the same is true in an Information Age economy—a disruption in the flow of information can have devastating global repercussions. All this is a reminder that while the Microchip Age is opening exciting new doors of economic growth and opportunity, it is also creating new risks and threats for which we must plan ahead.

THE NEW GLOBAL ECONOMY

Make no mistake: We are the leaders of the New Economy, and living in a global community has its rewards—namely, increased economic opportunity and prosperity for all Americans. But it also has its risks. In an age when capital and information can move around the world at the speed of light, so can sicknesses: When someone sneezes, everyone can get sick. And simply put, over the past several years, some of our neighbors have been quite sick indeed.

The sickness that turned into an economic crisis of global proportions began in Thailand during the summer of 1997. It spread through Southeast Asia, harming one country after another, including Japan, Hong Kong, South Korea, and Indonesia. But it didn't stop there. It also spread to an already troubled Russia and to Latin America, most notably Brazil, threatening to undo the enormous economic progress it has made in recent years.

How Washington handled the crisis has been instructive. First, it ignored the crisis. Then the government it was no big deal; it wouldn't affect us. Then, along with the IMF, the U.S. began throwing money at it, hoping it would go away. But worst of all, behind the scenes, the U.S. government and the IMF have offered these countries the worst possible advice, urging them to raise taxes and devalue their currencies. If your son or daughter was coming down with the flu, would you tell him or her to run outside without a coat on and lie down in the snow? This is essentially what the White House and the IMF told Asia, Russia, and Latin America to do, thus making matters worse, not better.

Fortunately, prudent, steady leadership came from the U.S. Federal Reserve, which lowered interest rates several times. Japan passed dramatic, Reaganesque tax cuts that are beginning to help the world's second largest economy begin the difficult path to economic recovery. American investors stayed calm and refused to pull out of the stock market. That helped keep the U.S. economy moving forward and bolstered the confidence of investors in other countries, too.

But all is not well. America cannot afford to be an island of prosperity in a sea of poverty. This global economic cancer may be in remission, but it could come back. To protect ourselves, and to show other countries how to get back on the road to healthy and sustained economic growth, we must take several important steps:

For starters, we need to inoculate the American economy by dramatically reducing and simplifying the tax burden, making it easier for Americans to save and invest and making it easier for businesses to remain profitable and keep creating jobs. This will give a huge shot in the arm to our own economy. It will also send the right message to other countries (like Russia) that the first step on the road to economic recovery is Reaganesque tax cuts and tax reform that put the people first, not the politicians.

We must also encourage American businesses and farmers by weeding out the excessive red tape that Washington has been creating over the past decade since President Reagan's departure from office. Regulations act as a hidden tax, and if we are not careful, they can begin to suffocate small businesses, destroy jobs, and choke off our economic growth.

We need real tort reform. Our courts are suffocating under the weight of frivolous lawsuits designed by greedy trial lawyers that bog down our legal system, drive up the cost of doing business, and hinder our economic competitiveness.

We need to open up markets where American goods and services are being discriminated against. It is time to blast away these trade barriers and give all Americans the freedom to compete and succeed in the emerging global marketplace.

We also need to keep the Federal Reserve from lurching into deflation or inflation. Remember, prosperity does not cause inflation. It's time to link the value of our money to something stable and secure, like the price of gold. That will ensure that the Fed does not inadvertently put its thumb on the world's windpipe, cause global currency turbulence, and cause commodity prices to be devastatingly low.

The bottom line is that while the enduring principles of economic progress may have escaped the politicians in Washington, they are very straightforward and we must once again remind ourselves of them and explain them to countries struggling through hard times: low taxes, low interest rates through sound money, property rights and the rule of law, open trade, and an environment in which small businesses can grow and flourish without overbearing bureaucratic interference. Never before has it been more important for us to get these fundamentals right, and help others to do the same, because the world is looking to us for answers. If we don't provide the right ones, who will?

CHAPTER ELEVEN

AMERICA IN THE
NEW MILLENNIUM

AS A NEW century and a new millennium dawn, Americans are entering an unprecedented Age of Opportunity. Sweeping economic, technological, and social changes are transforming the way we live and the way we work. The Cold War is over, the Information Revolution is upon us, and we are in the early stages of a new spiritual and moral awakening. Most Americans intuitively understand that a new era has arrived. Unfortunately, the professional politicians in Washington are still mired in old ideas and outdated solutions.

The twentieth century has been a century of big government, with its centralized structures and top-down bureaucracies. The twenty-first century, by contrast, is going to be the century of the family, a time of rediscovering the people and values that matter most in our lives. To truly make this possible, however, we must reform the political class and culture in Washington, so that money, power, and freedom are returned to the American people, to whom they rightfully belong. We must restore the promise of the American dream.

The marketplace is adjusting rapidly to this Age of Opportunity. E-commerce over the Internet, for example, is exploding. In 1993 only three million Americans were connected to the Internet. By 1999, that number had climbed to more than eighty million. On-line revenues have grown exponentially. At the same time, electronic communications have enabled more than twenty million Americans to leave behind long commutes and crowded offices in order to work at home. Today, our New Economy offers Americans previously unimaginable opportunities to shop for just what they want, pursue their hobbies and interests more easily than ever before, spend more time with their families, and access a seemingly limitless world of knowledge and information.

That's good news—an increasingly pro-family, pro-consumer economy that promises to bless us all. The bad news is that while the rest of American society is entering the Information Age, Washington is stuck in the Iron Age—decades behind the times. Our political leaders aren't seeking to meet the pressing needs of America's forgotten families. They aren't changing the way government does business in order to save families' time and money and give them more freedom, more choices, and more control over their own lives. Instead, they continue to take record amounts of our income, impose expensive and time consuming regulations (including the dreaded 1040 form), and undermine rather than reinforce the values that we hold dear.

Today we have a tax system that is too complex and too corrupt and forces working families to fork over huge amounts of time and money to the federal government. Why is there no serious effort to scrap the tax code and let all Americans keep a greater portion of their earnings? They surely know how to spend it better than the government.

We have a Social Security system that imposes a massive tax burden on families and young people but offers a dismal return on their money. It is a system that is heading for bankruptcy before our youngest workers reach retirement age. Why is there no concerted national effort to set seniors free from the fear that the system will fail them and to give younger workers the freedom to choose a new and better system of personal retirement accounts? Why do we let the federal government raid the Social Security Trust Fund to the tune of tens of billions of dollars a year in order to support wasteful spending by the rest of the government?

We have a health care system buried in expensive, counterproductive regulations that are driving up costs and forcing more and more working families (including children) into the ranks of the uninsured. Fewer and fewer families can choose their own doctor today. Why is there no serious national effort to pass a Health Care Declaration of Independence, dramatically expand affordable catastrophic insurance, and allow tax-free Medical Savings Accounts for those who need them most?

Today we have a grossly top-heavy, value-free education system that is failing to prepare millions of children to compete and succeed in the Age of Opportunity. Far too many American schools have low academic standards and little, if any, discipline in classrooms and hallways. Spending on education has risen sharply, while test scores and real learning have declined. Why not give parents the freedom to choose schools that work—schools that are safe, clean, and effective, and that reinforce rather than undermine the moral and spiritual values parents are trying to instill at home? Why not introduce healthy competition into the educational system, with a variety of schools available to parents, instead of letting the entrenched bureaucracy have a monopoly on the education of our children? Why not give teachers the freedom to create the best schools the world has ever seen?

Finally, we live in a dangerous world, with the threat of attack by nuclear, chemical, and biological weapons increasing daily. The Cold War has ended, but most national security specialists believe that the odds of a foreign or terrorist attack on American soil have increased, not declined. Why then have we let our armed forces deteriorate through excessive budget cuts? Why do we not resolve to have the finest, most robust, and most ready fighting forces in the world? And why is there no serious effort to deploy missile defense

systems that would protect our territory from attacks by the growing number of small states that will soon possess ballistic missiles?
The technology of missile defense is within our reach. All that is
needed is the will to move forward.

**Dramatic reforms are
needed, but none
occur. Why? Because
our politicians have
forgotten the meaning
of leadership.**

In all these areas, dramatic reforms are
needed, but none occur. Why? Because our
politicians have forgotten the meaning of
leadership. They use warm, fuzzy phrases and
poll-tested platitudes to promise change, but
year after year goes by and the status quo
remains essentially unchanged. The heart of
the problem is that Washington politicians
have caved in to special-interest groups who
shower them with campaign contributions. The number of lobbyists
in Washington has tripled over the past three decades to nearly
seventy thousand. In addition, there are now more than twelve
thousand special-interest groups doing business in our nation's capital, fighting to make real change impossible. We will never end
the morass of Washington by electing more career politicians. We
need independent, outsider, citizen candidates who will represent
the American people and the national interest, not their own careers
or narrowly partisan interests.

The presidential election in 2000 should be nothing less than a
dramatic national referendum to define America's future. Will "we
the people" take back our country from the entrenched politicians,
special interests, and lobbyists? Or will we continue to elect career
politicians who make promises only to break them, who stalwartly
defend the status quo, and who have no intention of setting families free from the excessive burden imposed by big government?

If we are to restore the values and vision that made America
great, it will require sweeping reforms in the way government works
and a return of power and resources to the American people. But
there is more. We must also bring about a spiritual and moral
reawakening, for this is the only sure foundation upon which a

rebirth of freedom is possible. John Adams believed similarly sentiment: "Our Constitution was made only for a moral and religious people. It is wholly inadequate to the government of any other."

The United States indeed has the best Constitution ever penned by mortal hand, but it is a Constitution whose success depends on a virtuous electorate and the leadership of men and women of integrity who are prepared, as the Founders, to pledges their lives, their fortunes, and their sacred honor to the cause of America. It is imperative that we elect such a leader in the year 2000, a leader who can restore and revitalize the American dream.

From the beginning, the American dream has flowed from the basic goodness and greatness of the American people. Government has either trusted and supported the people, or condescended to them, lectured them, and obstructed their God-given potential. But even at its best, government alone can never make a nation either good or great.

Will "we the people" take back our country from the entrenched politicians, special interests, and lobbyists? Or will we continue to elect career politicians who make promises only to break them?

It was not the machines of the twentieth century that made industrial America great. It was the men and women who conceived, built, and operated them. Nor will it be the computers and high technology of the next century that take us to new heights. Rather, it will be men and women who truly have been set free to discover and develop the spirit of enterprise and innovation to govern their own lives and raise their own families, free from the excesses of predatory government. The American dream is realized ultimately in the heart and soul of a free people. It flows from their highest aspirations, their talents and productivity, their hard work and determination.

The spirit of America is embodied in its soldiers and seamen who have defended this country valiantly from its inception, many at the price of their lives, and who defend it still today. Our servicemen deserve the finest of everything our laboratories and industry can produce, all that is needed to maintain the security of our shores and the tranquility of our nation. In the long run, the capability of our armed forces and the destiny of America are inextricably linked.

The spirit of America is found in its millions of farmers, laborers, and mechanics whose hard work makes possible the prosperity we all enjoy. We must free our working families from the heavy tax burden they bear, and give them access to a secure retirement and to health insurance that will free them from worry, not bury them in regulations and restrictions.

The spirit of America lies in the dynamism of our inventors, scientists, and entrepreneurs whose ingenuity and creativity have been a fount of national prosperity for over two centuries. It is no accident that almost every major technological breakthrough since 1800 has taken place in America. To name but a few: the light bulb, the automobile, manned flight, television, transistors and microprocessors, jet propulsion and rocketry, the polio vaccine, computers, and the Internet. Even today, the United States is awarded more international patents annually than all other industrial nations combined. This is what freedom can do. This is why our government must never encroach upon the freedom of its people to discover, explore, invest, and innovate.

The spirit of America lives in the hearts of true patriots and statesmen, great leaders who placed nation above self. There comes to mind the self-effacing sacrifice of George Washington, who led the Continental Army for seven years without a penny of pay. We remember Abraham Lincoln, whose unyielding fortitude saved a nation and brought freedom to millions; Teddy Roosevelt, who brought America onto the world stage; Franklin D. Roosevelt, who captained the greatest war ever fought; Harry Truman, who held firm against communist expansion when first it menaced the free world; Ronald Reagan, whose quiet courage brought an honorable end to the Cold War. There were also myriad Americans who held no office but whose lives transformed our world: Clara Barton, Henry Ford, Susan B. Anthony, Neil Armstrong, Jonas Salk, and countless others. And who can forget Jackie Robinson, Rosa Parks, and Martin Luther King, Jr., whose devotion to justice inspired a civil rights revolution to restore the dignity and worth of every American?

The spirit of America is the spirit of a nation of free people gatherered from the whole earth, a nation of immigrants from every land who, "yearning to breathe free," entered through the golden door to a land of endless promise. Our nation was built by people so devoted to freedom that they fled at great sacrifice from every imaginable form of tyranny overseas. With this as their legacy, Americans are and always have been the most independent-minded people on the face of the earth, a people stemming from all races and nationali-ties, but united in their allegiance to the Constitution and their deter-mination to live free, work free, and fight for freedom at any price.

This is the spirit of America. This is the American dream. It is a dream that extends far beyond our own shores. As Thomas Paine wrote in *Common Sense,* "The cause of America is in great measure the cause of all mankind." The future of America, more than any other single factor, will profoundly affect the future of freedom throughout the world.

As we enter the twenty-first century, two paths lie before us: We can continue down the road of top-heavy, stale government, while our national greatness declines, our creative energy is dissipated, and a once proud nation suffers moral and economic decline. Or "we the people" can revitalize the principles and hopes upon which the American republic was founded and bring about a new birth of free-dom in our land. We can restore our government to its rightful role; lift the burdens of excessive taxation and regulation from our people; lay a sound foundation for the fiscal security of future generations; promote industry, innovation, and entrepreneurship; rejuvenate our armed forces; and restore our society's commitment to family life and traditional moral values. There will be opposition and obstacles, setbacks and sacrifices. But with honest, visionary, determined lead-ership, it can be done. It must and will be done.

This is a vision of renewed freedom that can carry us triumphant into the new millennium, a people and nation worthy of the exalted name of "American." And daunting though the obstacles may appear, we shall prevail as we have always done in the past, for the simple reason that *we are Americans, born to be free.*

ACKNOWLEDGEMENTS

LIFE IS A team sport. Whether we are raising families, building companies, launching new ventures, or writing books, we all need a cadre of family and friends upon whose good humor, wise judgment, and limitless patience we can depend. In this, I have been greatly blessed.

My wife, Sabina, has been my best friend for nearly three decades and a wonderful mother to our five daughters—Roberta, Sabina, Catherine, Moira, and Elizabeth. She has taught us much, cared for us without limit, and endured a grueling schedule with a cheerful heart and a steady hand. We never envisioned a public life for ourselves or our kids, and we are still adjusting. But whatever we do, we do together, and I am deeply grateful for her love.

My brothers—Tim, Bob, Kip, and their wives—and my sister, Moira, and her husband have always been there to support, advise, challenge, and roast me. Believe it or not, I really am grateful. Thanks.

The entire *Forbes* team—led brilliantly through the years by editor Jim Michaels, and now being led to new heights by Bill Baldwin, Larry Minard, Cap Weinberger, Leonard Yablon, Rich Karlgaard, Brian Mulroney, and Domingo Cavallo—is the best in the business. They are committed to keeping our readers on the cutting edge, and I am proud to call them friends.

My executive assistant at *Forbes*, Jackie DeMaria, along with Maureen Murray-Hawes, Joan Cook, Merrill Vaughn, Maura Smith, and Scott Bistayi, are the most loyal, professional, and good-humored support team that anyone could hope for.

My chief political advisers, Bill Dal Col and John McLaughlin, have become like brothers to me. They believed in my vision for America when few else did. They have taken bullets for me, and with me, and never lost the faith. They are true entrepreneurs and risk-takers, sensing opportunities and seizing the moment, and have the kind of moxie I look for in business and in politics.

When it comes to innovative new ideas, so many people have been so generous with their time and insights over the years. I could not possibly list them all. But a few deserve particular thanks: Ronald and Nancy Reagan; Margaret and Dennis Thatcher; Milton and Rose Friedman; Ohio Secretary of State Ken Blackwell; Mayor Brett Schundler of Jersey City; Craig and Barbara Barrett; Herman Cain; John Herrington; Steve Merksemer; Alveda King; Peggy Noonan; Jack Kemp, Bill Bennett, Jeane Kirkpatrick, and the Empower America team; Lew Lehrman; Dick Gilder; Don Devine; Larry Kudlow; Rick Segal, Mike Hensley, and Tom Rentschler.

Also wonderfully helpful to me in developing the ideas in this book have been: Chris DeMuth and Michael Novak at the American Enterprise Institute; George Gilder and Bruce Chapman at the Discovery Institute; Walter Williams at George Mason University; Ed Feulner, Bridgett Wagner, Dan Mitchell, Bill Beach, Rae Hederman, Adam Meyerson, Joe Loconte, Stuart Butler, Bob Moffit, Nina Shokraii, Robert Rector, Kim Holmes, Jim Phillips, Rick Fisher, Baker Spring, and Ariel Cohen at the Heritage Foundation; Ed Crane, José Piñera, Mike Tanner, Darcy Olsen, Steve Moore, Jerry Taylor, and Ed Hudgins at the CATO Institute; Grace

Marie Arnett at the Galen Institute; Jeanne Allen at the Center for Education Reform; Armstrong Williams; Lisa Graham Keegan; David and Meredith Liben and Christina Giammalva at The Family Academy; Matt Glavin at the Southeastern Legal Foundation; Ron Unz and Gloria Matta Tuchman; Karen Kerrigan at the Small Business Survival Committee; John Raisian, Alvin Rabushka, and Thomas Sowell at the Hoover Institution; Kate O'Beirne and Dusty Rhodes at *National Review*; Sally Pipes at the Pacific Research Institute; Grover Norquist, Peter Ferrara, and Audrey Mullen at Americans for Tax Reform; Sam and Heather Beard at Economic Security 2000; Pat Rooney at Golden Rule Insurance; Fred Smith and Jonathan Adler at the Competitive Enterprise Institute; Gary and Aldonna Robbins of Fiscal Associates; Steve Entin at the Institute for Research on the Economics of Taxation; Alan Reynolds at the Hudson Institute; Richard Rahn at Novecon; Lew Uhler at the National Tax Limitation Committee; John Goodman, Merrill Matthews, and Bruce Bartlett of the National Center for Policy Analysis; William Guerrero and Robert DePosada at the Hispanic Business Roundtable; Paul Beckner and his team at Citizens for a Sound Economy; Patrick Fleenor at the Tax Foundation; Nina Shea at Freedom House; Richard Pipes at Harvard University; Daniel Pipes at *Middle East Quarterly*; Frank Gaffney and Rinelda Bliss at the Center for Security Policy; Edmund Peterson at Project 21; Patti and former Senator Gordon Humphrey; former Senator Malcolm Wallop; former Senator Bob Kasten; Ken Tomlinson; and Brent Bozell, Morton Blackwell, Paul Weyrich, and Keith Fournier, who have always been so gracious with their time and ideas.

Helping me communicate these ideas over the years have been: Greg Mueller, Lisa Kruska, Keith Appell, and Sean McCabe; Craig Shirley and Diana Banister; Norman Cohen; Jon Kraushar; Linda Pell; Clint Smullyen; Deroy Murdock; Al Herskovitz; Harry O'Connor; Ephram Zimbalist, Jr.; Bill Eisner; and Paul Sanderson.

I'm also deeply grateful to the team at Regnery Publishing, including Al Regnery, Jeff Carneal, Tom Phillips, Harry Crocker, and Erica Rogers. Thanks for your patience.

Finally, I'd like to say a special word of thanks to Joel Rosenberg, Dr. Bruce Porter, Clark Judge, and Josh Gilder, who over the past several years have worked closely with me on this and other projects. Without their insights and persistence, this book never would have happened. It is better for all the hard work they have invested.

ABOUT THE AUTHOR

STEVE FORBES IS a successful chief executive and international business leader who understands how to keep America strong and prosperous as we head into the twenty-first century.

In 1996, Steve stunned political pundits and the Washington establishment by winning upset Republican primaries in Delaware and Arizona. He won with a positive, forward-looking, inclusive vision to give every American the freedom to participate in this new era of prosperity.

Steve is also a family man, a devoted husband of twenty-eight years and the father of five daughters. He knows firsthand the challenge of raising children in a culture where it seems, at times, as though the wheels are coming off. He has written and spoken thoughtfully and without apology about how to rebuild "The Moral Basis of a Free Society."

In 1990, Steve became president and CEO of Forbes, Inc., and editor-in-chief of *Forbes*. Under Steve's leadership, the company has sought to keep readers on the cutting edge of the enormous changes under way in the American economy on the eve of the twenty-first century. New magazines launched under Steve's direction include *Forbes ASAP*, focusing on people shaping the high-tech, Information Age economy; *Forbes Digital Tool*, an on-line business magazine; and *American Legacy*, focusing on the people shaping African-American history and culture. As a result of Steve's leadership, *Forbes* is now the world's foremost business magazine.

For three decades, Steve has traveled extensively throughout the U.S., personally writing about the people and ideas shaping the future. He has emerged as a leader and an innovator of new strategies to expand individual opportunity and economic security. Such strategies include a new Social Security system of personal retirement accounts for young people; a flat tax that's honest, simple, and a real tax cut for working families; Medical Savings Accounts; and parental control of education.

A respected voice on foreign policy and national security issues, Steve has worked closely with presidents, prime ministers, and business leaders in more than sixty countries. President Reagan named Steve Forbes chairman of the bipartisan Board for International Broadcasting in 1985 to communicate a message of free markets and free elections behind the Iron Curtain. As chairman, Steve oversaw the operation of Radio Free Europe and Radio Liberty, whose broadcasts were praised by Poland's Lech Walesa as being critical to the struggle against communism. Steve was reappointed to the post by President Bush and served until April of 1993.

Sensing a serious vacuum of pro-growth, pro-freedom leadership in the 1996 Republican presidential primaries, Steve entered the race and ran an unconventional, outsider campaign. Starting as an asterisk in the polls, Steve and his message of "hope, growth, and opportunity" conservatism quickly captured the imagination of the American people. *Time* and *Newsweek* ran cover stories on Steve and his message, Steve and his family were profiled on *60 Minutes*, and he was widely credited with reshaping the national debate.

In August of 1996, Steve launched Americans for Hope, Growth, and Opportunity, a national issue advocacy organization, to continue building support for his positive, forward-looking agenda. Steve served as honorary chairman, and *Business Week* dubbed the group "the nation's first message tank." The group ran over sixty radio ad campaigns and five TV ad campaigns on issues ranging from saving Social Security to building a missile defense system to scrapping the tax code. It operated English and Spanish-language websites and produced a daily radio commentary program heard on over 160 stations nationwide.

Steve has also communicated his visionary message in speeches all over the country and on regular appearances on national newsmaker programs. In addition, he has guest-hosted *Saturday Night Live* and appeared on *The Tonight Show with Jay Leno* and *The Late Show with David Letterman*.

Steve Forbes has long been personally interested and involved in trying to remove the barriers that stand in the way of working families to achieve their dreams. From 1993 to 1996, he was chairman of Empower America, a grassroots reform organization founded by Jack Kemp, Bill Bennett, and Jeane Kirkpatrick.

Steve serves on the board of numerous public policy organizations, including the Ronald Reagan Presidential Foundation, the National Taxpayers Union, and the American Enterprise Institute. He is also on the Board of Trustees of Princeton University, and is on the Board of Overseers of the Memorial Sloan-Kettering Cancer Center in New York.

Steve was born on July 18, 1947, in Morristown, New Jersey. He graduated from Princeton University in 1970 with a bachelor's degree in history, and served for five-and-a-half years in the New Jersey National Guard. He currently resides in Bedminster, New Jersey. He and his wife, Sabina, have five daughters: Roberta, Sabina, Catherine, Moira, and Elizabeth.

INDEX